Danish

Cooking and Baking Traditions

THE HIPPOCRENE COOKBOOK LIBRARY

Afghan Food & Cookery
Alps, Cuisines of the
Aprovecho: A Mexican-American Border
  Cookbook
Argentina Cooks!, Exp. Ed.
Belarusian Cookbook, The
Bolivian Kitchen, My Mother's
Brazil: A Culinary Journey
Cajun Cuisine, Stir the Pot: The History of
Cajun Women, Cooking with
Calabria, Cucina di
Chile, Tasting
China's Fujian Province, Cooking from
Colombian Cooking, Secrets of
Corsican Cuisine
Croatian Cooking, Best of, Exp. Ed.
Czech Cooking, Best of, Exp. Ed.
Danish Cooking and Baking Traditions
Danube, All Along The, Exp. Ed.
Emilia-Romagna, The Cooking of
Egyptian Cuisine and Culture, Nile Style:
English Country Kitchen, The
Estonian Tastes and Traditions
Filipino Food, Fine
Finnish Cooking, Best of
Germany, Spoonfuls of
Greek Cooking, Regional
Haiti, Taste of
Havana Cookbook, Old (Bilingual)
Hungarian Cookbook, Exp. Ed.
India, A Culinary Journey
India, Flavorful
International Dictionary of Gastronomy
Jewish-Iraqi Cuisine, Mama Nazima's
Kerala Kitchen, The
Laotian Cooking, Simple
Lebanese Cookbook, The

Ligurian Kitchen, A
Lithuanian Cooking, Art of
Malaysia, Flavors of
Middle Eastern Kitchen, The
Naples, My Love for
Nepal, Taste of
New Hampshire: from Farm to Kitchen
New Jersey Cookbook, Farms and Foods
  of the Garden State:
Ohio, Farms and Foods of
Persian Cooking, Art of
Pied Noir Cookbook: French Sephardic
  Cuisine
Piemontese, Cucina: Cooking from Italy's
  Piedmont
Polish Cooking, Best of, Exp. Ed.
Polish Heritage Cookery, Ill. Ed.
Polish Holiday Cookery
Polish Traditions, Old
Portuguese Encounters, Cuisines of
Punjab, Menus and Memories from
Romania, Taste of
Russian Cooking, The Best of
Scottish-Irish Pub and Hearth Cookbook
Sephardic Israeli Cuisine
Sicilian Feasts
Slovenia, Flavors of
South Indian Cooking, Healthy
Spain, La Buena Mesa: The Regional
  Cooking of
Trinidad and Tobago, Sweet Hands:
  Island Cooking from
Turkish Cuisine, Taste of
Tuscan Kitchen, Tastes from a
Ukrainian Cuisine, Best of, Exp. Ed.
Uzbek Cooking, Art of
Warsaw Cookbook, Old

Danish

Cooking and Baking Traditions

ARTHUR L. MEYER

Illustrations by John A. Wilson

HIPPOCRENE BOOKS, INC.

New York

Color photography by Arthur L. Meyer.

Book and jacket design by Wanda España/Wee Design Group.

For more information, address:
HIPPOCRENE BOOKS, INC.
171 Madison Avenue
New York, NY 10016
www.hippocrenebooks.com

Library of Congress Cataloging-in-Publication Data

Meyer, Arthur L.
Danish cooking and baking traditions / by Arthur L. Meyer.
p. cm.
Culinary terms in Danish and English.
Includes index.
ISBN-13: 978-0-7818-1262-7 (hardcover)
ISBN-10: 0-7818-1262-3 (hardcover)
1. Cooking, Danish. 2. Baking. 3. Cookbooks. I. Title.
TX722.D4M49 2011
641.8'659--dc23
2011016722

For the Bechtold Family

He who has plenty of butter, may put some in his cabbage.

—a Danish Proverb

Contents

Introduction

Danish cuisine is a cuisine of the country, of small farms and locally produced foods. Travel was difficult in the early days, and so trade between villages and other regions was limited. Danes needed to make do with what they could raise and produce on their farms. Considering the long winters and lack of refrigeration, preservation was very important. To this day, Danish cuisine is rich in smoked, pickled, and salted foods. Some of the world's finest dairy can be found in Denmark and its butter and cheeses are examples of food preservation taken to the highest culinary level. Long winters also dictate the availability of fruits and vegetables year-round. Root vegetables, such as potatoes, celery root, and beets, store well in cold cellars over the winter, as do cabbages and other cruciferous crops. Apples are enjoyed year-round for the same reason. Cold weather-friendly fruits such as berries are also part of the Danish food table, as sauces to accompany meats and as delicate jellies and puddings for desserts and pastries.

Typically, Danish recipes are quite filling and rich. Most are based on dairy and are high in calories. There is a trend for modern Danish cooks to trim fat and incorporate more fresh vegetables, but traditional Danish fare still demands copious amounts of butter and cream. It is this reliance on exquisite dairy products that allows Danish bakers to produce the most delicious pastries, cookies, and cakes. To this day, baking is a tradition passed down through generations, and home-baked breads, especially sour rye and pumpernickel, are part of every meal. *Smørrebrød*, the famous open sandwiches of Denmark, are based on these wonderfully hearty and flavorful breads.

Impeccably fresh fish, pork, and dairy, with little interference from herbs and spices, flavor the cuisine. The occasional bay leaf, pinch of sage, or sprig of dill will suffice to complement a recipe, but assertive spices are not part of the Danish food palette. Danes do enjoy the bright flavors of pickling, and the acidic notes of vinegar and lemon juice are common. Salted foods, especially fish and pork, complete the intensity of Danish cuisine. Bold spices come into play with Danish baked goods, where the citrus perfume of cardamom and the seductive spiciness of cinnamon and clove make their statement.

The Land and People

The name Denmark came into use during the 9th century (*Danmark* meaning "border of the Danes"). The Romans had the most influence on the region before then and the Vikings explored and conquered from Denmark beginning in the 800s. It was Viking influence that brought Denmark into association with Europe. Profitable trade was established that continues to this day. By the 1300s Denmark was considered a great European power. Denmark's boundaries today are the result of loss in territory by siding with Napoleonic France in the early 1800s, by losing a war with Prussia in 1864, and by declaring neutrality during World War I.

Denmark consists of a large peninsula called Jutland, bordering Germany to the south, and numerous islands of varying size. Copenhagen, Denmark's capital, is on the large island of Zealand. Approximately 70 percent of Denmark's land is arable, and food products comprise the largest portion of the manufacturing economy of Denmark. Danish hams and pork products, as well as butter, are shipped worldwide and are considered superior quality. When it comes to quality, Danish dairy products have no equal.

The climate is surprisingly temperate for Denmark's latitude as it is subtly warmed by the Gulf Stream. Winters are long and dark and temperatures average around 30 degrees F, and in the 60s during the very brief summer. Growing seasons are short, so vegetables that can be quickly grown need to hold up well over prolonged periods in cold storage. Making butter and cheese from the rich milk of dairy cows is an excellent way to preserve dairy over long winters as well. The land is flat, making it relatively easy to farm, and the many streams and rivers carved out by ancient glacial action furnish needed water.

Greenland and the Faeroe Islands were part of Denmark from the 14th century until the Faeroe Islands gained independence in 1948 and Greenland in 1978, but Danish is still their official language. Because of isolation due to remoteness, harsh climate, and poor soil, Faeroe Island cuisine has been based on what was available and could be preserved. Raw meats and fish can be preserved by air drying, and the salty atmosphere prevents rotting. Meats hung for several months are called *ræstkjøt*, and those hung for a year or more *skerpikjøt*, which is eaten raw. Fish and whale meat that is air dried for short and long periods are called *ræstanfisk* and *turranfisk*, respectively.

Traditional Greenland cuisine is also that of local availability. Expect seal, whale, sea bird, and reindeer meat to be the focus of the meal. A classic soup called *suaasat* includes these meats and onions and potatoes, with little seasoning except for salt and pepper. Lunch and snack time favor dried cod with whale blubber. A most prized delicacy is *mattak*, a combination of dried reindeer meat and whale skin with blubber. In the fall, wild blueberries and crowberries accompany dried meats and form the foundation of simple desserts.

To understand the Danes, one must understand a term heard constantly during conversation. *Hygge*, and the adjective form *hyggelig*, is the essence and soul of Danish life. As with many foreign language terms, it is impossible to define *hygge* with one word or sentence. *Hygge* is an experience of feeling comfortable and at ease in a friendly environment. It is often associated with food and friendly gatherings, but may also describe a sofa. Informal, cozy, and

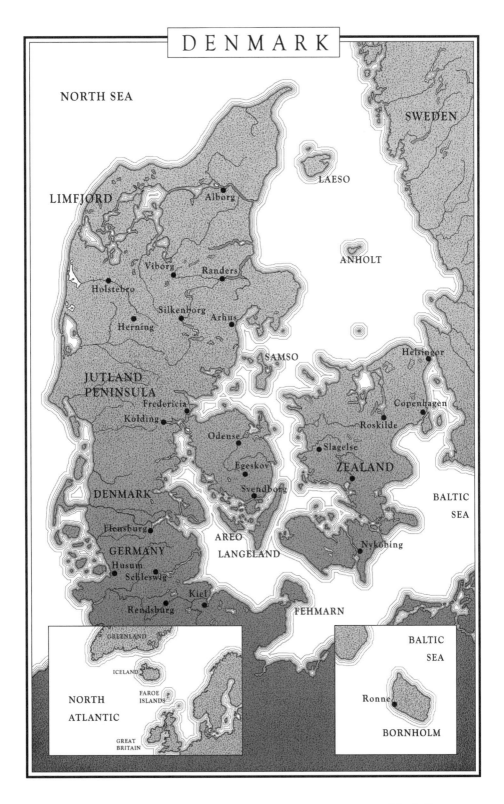

DENMARK

NORTH SEA

SWEDEN

LIMFJORD

LAESO

Alborg

ANHOLT

Viborg

Randers

Holstebro

Silkenborg

Arhus

Herning

SAMSO

Helsingor

JUTLAND
PENINSULA

Fredericia

Copenhagen

Kolding

Roskilde

Odense

Slagelse

Egeskov

ZEALAND

Svendborg

DENMARK

BALTIC
SEA

Flensburg

AREO

Nykobing

GERMANY

LANGELAND

Husum

Schleswig

Kiel

Rendsburg

FEHMARN

GREENLAND

BALTIC
SEA

ICELAND

NORTH

FAROE
ISLANDS

Ronne

ATLANTIC

BORNHOLM

GREAT
BRITAIN

uncomplicated are words that also touch on its meaning. As explained to me by a long-time resident of Helsingor, *hyggelig* is a way of being and a state of mind that is always with them in every situation. Social interaction is dictated by the doctrine of *Janteloven*, where hubris, bragging, and personal recognition are frowned upon. It is based on the long-held Danish tradition of equality among the masses.

Danes enjoy one of the world's highest standards of living, and are taxed accordingly. Medicine has been socialized for many years, and compulsory education has been in place since the mid-19th century; the literacy rate is virtually 100 percent among adults. Denmark's population, which has remained steady over the years and is not projected to grow in the near future, is about 5,400,000 people. Copenhagen, Århus, and Odense are the three most populous cities, accounting for almost 30 percent of the total population, and are centers for Denmark's new *garde* chefs. Here you will find daring individuals bringing New World chiles, Thai fish sauce, roasted garlic, and wasabi to the innocent and naïve palates of metropolitan Denmark, tantalizing their taste buds with more flavor and less fat.

One notable dining habit of metropolitan Danes is their love for hot dogs, especially as street food. The sausage carts, called *pølsevogn*, are towed behind small scooters and are then set up on the street to do business. Served with mustard and ketchup on the side, Danes will dip the thin, long hot dogs, called *røda pølsa*, into these sauces using fingers and napkin to grasp the sausage at one end. Bread is optional and condiments such as remoulade sauce or grilled onions are available upon request.

Ingredients

The most important aspect of Danish cuisine is the quality of the ingredients used, especially dairy and pork. Butter and cheese are excellent ways to preserve a bountiful yield of milk, and the better the milk, the higher the quality of butter and cheese. Preserving meats, such as in making hams, bacon, and sausages, allow Denmark's superior pork products to transport more easily and last year-round. Denmark is blessed with ample grazing land and the right amount of rain for lush pastures. Cows and pigs are pampered and constantly inspected for health-related problems.

Before the 16th century, butter and cheese were important tithes to the king, and by the 19th century, cooperatives were being set up that would allow for increased technology and modern equipment. This shifted the profile of exporting goods from grain to dairy and Danish butter and cheese became world-renowned for their superiority. At the World Exhibition of 1879 in London, Danish butter was given the highest award of quality. Today almost 97 percent of all Danish dairy is supplied by cooperatives that are strictly regulated to meet the highest standards in the industry.

Cheeses made in Denmark reflect the cuisine nicely. They are not strong and rely on the quality of ingredients. Danish cheeses are very buttery and mild tasting as a rule. The most recognizable Danish cheese worldwide is Havarti. When added cream enriches the culture, the product is called Cream Havarti. It slices well and makes a tasty addition to any sandwich, and is certainly high on the list of additions to *Smørrebrød*. Blue cheeses, such as Danablu, Saga, Blue Castello, and the more recently-developed Black Castello (in which the dark mold is not rinsed from the surface of the cheese), while not as sophisticated as the great blue cheeses of the world, are delicious and quite interesting nonetheless. Danablu is the quintessential crumbled cheese for salad, while the others can have a brie-like soft texture when young. Danbo, Esram, Fynbo, Maribo, Molbo, and Samso round out the offerings of traditional Danish cheeses, all typically made from cow's milk. Variations may include added herbs, garlic, onion, and even the more daring jalapeño.

Cooperative systems also control pork production, in place since the end of the 19th century. Denmark exports about 85 percent of its pork and has captured more than 20 percent of the total world market. The Danish canned ham is recognized and sold world-wide, as is Danish bacon, which resembles Canadian bacon. Fresh pork spareribs are exported primarily to the U.S. and all cuts of fresh Danish pork are sought out in Britain and continental Europe.

Danes treat their livestock humanely and in a healthy manner. Danish pork producers have banned the use of growth hormones and frivolous antibiotic usage, both of which become necessary when pen crowding and neglect are commonplace. Breeding has much to do with quality and Danish pigs are the result of careful breeding practices. Having a distinct physical appearance the Danish Landrace pig is a medium-size breed without excess fat or wrinkles, and appears to be the ideal animal bred for superior pork products. Interestingly, the Landrace is required to be bred with the Great White pig in Italy to produce world famous prosciutto di Parma hams.

Danish cuisine is wholesome and the ingredients are of the finest quality. Danish cooks believe, as do most good chefs, that if you start with the best possible ingredients and prepare them simply, the outcome is guaranteed. Baking is so much a part of this cuisine that a separate section is devoted to it in this book, and it adheres to this philosophy. The freshest milk and cream combined with highest quality butter, eggs from contented chickens, and freshly ground spices must produce baked goods that are world-renowned.

Part 1

Cooking Traditions

Soups

Danish soups are hearty fare. Usually they are not meant to be a prelude to a filling meal—they are the meal itself. Rich in meats and vegetables, soups are frequently served for dinner during the long winter months. Meatballs and forcemeat are an important part of Danish cuisine and these make delicate additions to a rich broth. Dried legumes and peas, easy to store over the winter, along with cabbage, potatoes, and other winter-friendly vegetables are welcome additions to a comforting bowl of soup.

More refreshing and less filling are the fruit soups enjoyed throughout Denmark. They usually begin or end the meal, and are most often served hot. Cold fruit soups are dessert fare, topped with rich whipped cream, and are also used as palate cleansers to refresh the taste buds.

Winter Split Pea Soup (Gule Ærter)

Fresh Green Pea Soup (Grønaertesuppe)

Potato Soup (Kartoffelsuppe)

Beet Soup (Rødbedesuppe)

Cabbage Soup (hvidkaalssuppe)

Green Kale Soup (Grønkaalssuppe)

Cauliflower Soup (Blomkaalssuppe)

Chervil Soup (Kørvelsuppe)

Rice Porridge (Risengrød)

Bread and Beer Soup (Øllebrød)

Curry Soup (Karrysuppe)

Buttermilk Soup (Kærnemælksuppe)

Meat Soup (Kødsuppe)

Soup Dumplings (Melboller)

Forcemeat Dumplings for Soup (Kødboller)

Fruit Soup (Sød Suppe)

Apple Soup (Æblesuppe)

Cold Cherry Soup (Kirsebær Kold Skål)

Winter Split Pea Soup

Gule Ærter

This is Denmark's traditional winter soup, which is often cooked and served with pork or ham, Denmark's most famous food product. It's easy to prepare and inexpensive, yet it is considered more than common fare.

---

1 pound yellow split peas

2 pounds boneless pork shoulder, cut into 1-inch cubes

4 medium carrots, peeled and cut into 1-inch pieces

1 medium onion, quartered

1 medium celery root, peeled and cut into 1-inch pieces

1 sprig thyme

1 bay leaf

1 pound new potatoes, peeled and cut into 1-inch pieces

salt and pepper

Advance Preparation: Soak the peas in sufficient water overnight. Drain and discard the soaking liquid.

1. Add the pork cubes to 8 cups water in a large stockpot. Toss in the carrots, onion, celery root, thyme, and bay leaf. Simmer until the pork is tender, about 1 hour.

2. While the meat is cooking, in a separate pot simmer the soaked split peas in 6 cups water until soft, about 40 minutes.

3. Add the potatoes to the pork and cook an additional 10 minutes. Remove the meat and vegetables from the cooking liquid and reserve, discarding the herbs. Keep the cooking liquid in the pot.

4. Purée the peas with the reserved carrots and onion, using some of the cooking liquid to form a smooth mixture.

5. Add the pea purée to the reserved cooking liquid and stir. Toss in the pork, celery root, and potatoes and simmer 10 minutes. Adjust seasoning with salt and pepper.

6. Serve the soup with the pork removed to a separate plate.

Notes: Tangy mustard traditionally accompanies the pork. Low sodium ham may replace the pork shoulder. For a soup without pork, use a hambone in the split pea cooking liquid, cook the vegetables with the split peas and use that liquid as the base for the soup.

Fresh Green Pea Soup

Grønaertesuppe

This soup extols the bounty of the summer garden, with freshly shelled peas as its featured ingredient. The use of the shucked pods for additional flavor is interesting and not commonly seen elsewhere.

---

1 pound fresh green peas in pods

1 sprig dill

1 sprig parsley

4 medium potatoes, peeled and thinly sliced

3 medium carrots, peeled and sliced

3 tablespoons butter

2 tablespoons all-purpose flour

salt and pepper to taste

chopped parsley

Advance Preparation: Shuck the peas. Reserve them and save the pods for broth. In a large saucepan add the pods, dill, and parsley to 4 cups water and simmer over low heat 30 minutes. Strain and reserve the pea-pod broth.

1. Add the potatoes to 8 cups cold water in a large stockpot. Bring to a boil and lower the heat to a simmer. Cook over low heat until the potatoes begin to fall apart, about 10 minutes.

2. Add the carrots and reserved peas and cook an additional 5 minutes, stirring occasionally to break up the potatoes which are meant to thicken the soup. Stir in the reserved pea-pod broth.

3. Knead 2 tablespoons of the butter with the flour and add portions to the soup, whisking continuously to thicken it more. Adjust seasoning with salt and pepper.

4. To serve, add the soup to a tureen and top with the remaining tablespoon of butter. Sprinkle with parsley and serve immediately.

Notes: In a pinch, frozen peas can be used for this dish, replacing the pea-pod broth with water. Under no circumstances should canned peas be used for this recipe.

Potato Soup

Kartoffelsuppe

A traditional way to prepare soups in Denmark is to poach meats in water to make the base for the soup, and then serve the meats separately with horseradish sauce.

1½ pounds boneless veal shoulder or beef chuck

4 large russet potatoes, peeled and thinly sliced

2 medium onions, diced

2 leeks, white and light green parts only, thoroughly washed and sliced

4 tablespoons butter

1 bay leaf

2 sprigs parsley

1 cup dry white wine

½ cup heavy cream

salt and white pepper to taste

horseradish sauce (optional, see page 130)

Advance Preparation: In a large stockpot, poach the veal or beef in 6 cups water until tender, about 1 hour. Remove the meat from the cooking liquid and reserve both.

1. In a large skillet, sauté the potatoes, onions, and leeks in the butter over low heat for 10 minutes. Add these to the reserved cooking liquid. Toss in the bay leaf and parsley. Simmer, uncovered, 30 minutes over low heat.

2. Remove the bay leaf. Purée the soup and pass it through a sieve. Add the wine and cream. Simmer 5 minutes.

3. Adjust seasoning with salt and pepper. Slice the meat and serve separately with horseradish sauce, if using.

Notes: Veal is often used in this recipe. Fresh pork shoulder would be a tasty substitute for the beef.

Beet Soup

Rødbedesuppe

Beets are enjoyed across Scandinavia and Eastern Europe. Served cold with a dollop of sour cream, this recipe may remind you of Russian *borscht*.

12 large beets, washed and well scrubbed (do not peel them), cut into chunks

2 pounds beef short ribs

juice of 4 lemons

½ cup sugar

½ teaspoon allspice

1 medium red onion, sliced

salt and pepper to taste

sour cream

Advance Preparation: The entire recipe should be made in advance of serving to allow time for the soup to thoroughly chill.

1. Put the prepared beets in a large stockpot along with the short ribs, lemon juice, sugar, allspice, and sliced onion. Cover the contents with water and simmer covered for 1 hour, adding water as necessary.

2. Remove the short ribs and reserve for another use.

3. Purée the soup and pass it through a sieve. Adjust seasoning with salt and pepper.

4. Chill thoroughly and serve with dollops of sour cream.

Notes: For additional texture, some of the cooked beets may be finely diced and added to the purée. For a heartier version, trim and chop the meat from the cooked short ribs and add to the soup.

Cabbage Soup

Serves 8

Hvidkaalssuppe

This soup is often served with small meatballs. In another version of cabbage soup, the cabbage is first very slowly browned with sugar in a skillet (*Brunkålssuppe*).

---

2 pounds veal shanks

2 large onions, diced

1 head green cabbage, trimmed and coarsely chopped

6 tablespoons butter

4 carrots, peeled and sliced

4 medium new potatoes, diced

1 bay leaf

salt and pepper to taste

Advance Preparation: In a large stockpot, simmer the veal shanks in 8 cups water for 1 hour, or until tender. Remove the veal shanks and trim the meat from the bones and any marrow in the bones. Reserve the cooking liquid.

1. In a large skillet, sauté the onions and cabbage in butter until the onions are translucent and the cabbage has released its liquid, about 10 minutes.

2. Add these, along with the carrots and potatoes, to the reserved cooking liquid. Chop the reserved meat and marrow and add them to the liquid. Toss in the bay leaf and simmer the soup for 1 hour over low heat, partially covered, adding water as necessary.

3. When done, remove the bay leaf and adjust seasoning with salt and pepper. Serve piping hot.

Notes: Other meats, such as short ribs or country-style pork ribs, may replace the veal shanks. The cabbage may be browned with a little sugar before adding to the liquid.

Green Kale Soup

Grønkaalssuppe

Kale is an important garden vegetable and is a member of the cabbage family. It is rich in nutrients and antioxidants, grows well in all types of soil, and thrives in cold weather. It is said that kale becomes sweeter and more tender after a frost.

---

3 pounds pork shanks or ribs

1 tablespoon sugar

1 teaspoon salt

3 carrots, peeled and cut into cubes

2 medium onions, diced

2 medium new potatoes, cubed

2 celery ribs, cut into small pieces

3 cups chopped kale, washed and coarse spines removed from the leaves

salt and pepper to taste

Advance Preparation: In a large stockpot, simmer the pork in 8 cups water with the sugar and salt for 2 hours, skimming the surface as necessary. Remove the pork and reserve for another use. Reserve the pork stock.

1. Add the carrots, onions, potatoes, and celery to the pork stock. Simmer 1 hour partially covered.

2. Add the chopped kale and continue to simmer an additional 20 minutes, or until the kale is tender.

3. Adjust seasoning with salt and pepper and serve hot.

Notes: Some versions of this soup include barley. Cook ½ cup medium pearl barley in sufficient water until tender, about 45 minutes. Add this to the soup with the chopped kale.

Cauliflower Soup

Blomkaalssuppe

It is said that the ability to grow a good-quality cauliflower is the measure of a well-maintained garden. This plant is known to be the fussiest of the *Brassica* family (that also includes cabbage, broccoli, and kale). If the weather is too warm no heads will form, if too cold the heads will be small.

---

1 head cauliflower, leaves and stalk trimmed, cut into uniform, small florets

4 tablespoons butter

¼ cup all-purpose flour

6 cups chicken stock

½ cup dry white wine

4 egg yolks

1 tablespoon sugar

salt and pepper to taste

Advance Preparation: Steam (or simmer) the cauliflower florets until tender but not soft, about 8 minutes.

1. Melt the butter over low heat in a stockpot. Whisk in the flour and cook the roux for several minutes, whisking and being careful not to brown the mixture.

2. Whisk in the stock and wine, and cook over medium heat until it begins to simmer. Lower the heat and simmer 2 minutes.

3. Beat the egg yolks with the sugar. Whisk in a few tablespoons of hot soup to temper the yolks, and then whisk this into the simmering soup. Cook over low heat 2 minutes.

4. Add the steamed cauliflower and simmer over very low heat 2 minutes. Serve immediately.

Notes: For a tasty spinach soup, replace the cauliflower with 1 pound spinach that has been sautéed, chopped, and drained of excess liquid.

Chervil Soup

Serves 6

Kørvelsuppe

Unlike most herbs, chervil appreciates cool, moist, and shady areas. It is related to parsley and carrots, and the feathery leaves of chervil have a slight licorice note. Preserve its delicate flavor by adding it at the end of a recipe.

6 cups chicken or pork stock	salt and white pepper to taste
2 medium carrots, peeled and sliced	⅓ cup finely chopped fresh chervil,
4 tablespoons butter	about 1 large bunch (see Note)
¼ cup all-purpose flour	

Advance Preparation: All advance preparation may be found in the ingredient list.

1. In a large saucepan, heat the stock to a simmer and add the sliced carrots. Cook over low heat until the carrots are tender but not soft, about 5 minutes.

2. Melt the butter over low heat in another large saucepan. Whisk in the flour and cook the roux over low heat for several minutes, whisking and being careful not to brown the mixture.

3. Add the stock and carrots to the roux, stirring constantly. Bring to a boil and then lower the heat to a simmer. Cook 2 to 3 minutes. Adjust seasoning with salt and pepper.

4. Stir in the chopped chervil and serve immediately.

Notes: The chervil may be chopped in a food processor but be careful not to purée it. A traditional way to present this soup is to place a poached egg in each bowl before ladling in the soup.

Rice Porridge

Risengrød

A generous lump of cold butter is pressed into this hot porridge just before serving, allowing for a constant supply of melted butter to accompany each spoonful of rice. When fancied up with sugar and cinnamon, then topped with cream, it is known as *Julerisengrød*, Christmas rice pudding (see page 211 for the recipe).

---

1 cup raw rice   salt to taste
8 cups whole milk   cold butter

Advance Preparation: Blanch the rice in boiling water for 2 minutes. Drain thoroughly. Discard the liquid.

1. Heat the milk to a boil and add the rice. Lower the heat, cover, and simmer very slowly, for about 1 hour. More milk may be added if the porridge gets too thick. Stir and add salt to taste.

2. Serve portions of porridge with a generous piece of cold butter pressed into the center of each bowl.

Notes: Ground cinnamon and sugar may be sprinkled over the porridge for an added treat.

Copenhagen Cooking (also known as the Nordic Food Festival) is the annual tribute to Scandinavian food held in Denmark's capital. It is the largest festival of this kind in Scandinavia. Based on the tradition of Christian IV's coronation feast where oxen were cooked in various squares within the city, a large ox is roasted in Gråbrødretorv Square by the cooperative efforts of notable Copenhagen restaurants. Chunks of roasted ox accompanied by salad and buttered bread are offered for sale. As well, a variety of ethnic restaurants set up a street kitchen to sell an assortment of tasty treats. The festival is typically held in the last two weeks of August, but in 2011, the first Winter edition of the festival was launched in February.

Bread and Beer Soup

Øllebrød

This soup is one recipe that must appear in any Danish cookbook but also may be the most difficult to reproduce outside Denmark. The beer used is called *hvidtøl*, a malty, very low alcohol, very sweet ale-style beer.

---

10 ounces (about 8 thick slices) pumpernickel rye bread, torn into small pieces

2 cups wheat beer (*weissbier* or white beer)

1 cup porter or stout

⅓ cup sugar

juice and grated zest of 1 lemon

heavy cream

Advance Preparation: In a large bowl, soak the bread in the beer, stout, and 1 cup water for several hours or overnight.

1. In a large saucepan, slowly bring the bread and beer mixture to a boil, stirring occasionally. Cook over low heat until the bread breaks up and forms a thick soup.

2. Pass the soup through a coarse strainer or sieve and heat the soup again over low heat.

3. Add the sugar, lemon juice and zest. Stir to dissolve the sugar. Cook 2 minutes.

4. Serve soup in bowls drizzled with cream.

Notes: For special occasions a dollop of whipped cream replaces the heavy cream in this recipe. If *hvidtøl* is available, use 3 cups in place of the wheat beer and stout.

Curry Soup

Karrysuppe

Curry powder is one of the few "exotic" spices found in Scandinavian cuisine and is quite popular. In Norway and Sweden the base for this soup is meat stock, but in Denmark it is usually fish stock.

---

8 cups fish stock (see Advance Preparation)

3 tablespoons butter

1 small onion, sliced

2 garlic cloves, minced

1 Granny Smith apple, peeled, cored, and grated

1 teaspoon curry powder

1 sprig fresh thyme

3 tablespoons all-purpose flour

½ cup heavy cream

Advance Preparation: The fish stock may be made from leftover shrimp shells, scraps of trimmed fish, or a whole fish that has been cleaned. Add the fish scraps to 9 cups cold water in a stockpot and slowly bring to a boil. Lower the heat and simmer 20 minutes, skimming occasionally. Strain and discard the fish.

1. Heat the butter in a large stockpot. Add the sliced onion and sauté 2 minutes over low heat, being careful not to brown the onions.

2. Stir in the garlic, grated apple, curry powder, thyme, and flour. Cook over low heat 5 minutes.

3. Whisk in the fish stock. Cook over medium heat for several minutes, allowing the soup to briefly come to a boil.

4. Stir in the cream and serve at once.

Notes: Vegetable stock may be substituted for the fish stock. A small amount of bottled clam juice may be added to this. Adjust the amount of curry powder according to taste; consider using hot curry powder for a non-traditional boost in spiciness.

Buttermilk Soup

Kærnemælksuppe

Traditional buttermilk is the fermented liquid remaining after butter is churned from cream. Danish dairies produce some of the world's finest butter, and so it should come as no surprise that there is always a plentiful supply of superior grade buttermilk for cooking and baking.

½ cup raisins	juice and grated zest of 1 lemon
½ cup orange juice	pinch salt
¼ cup all-purpose flour	¼ teaspoon cinnamon
8 cups (2 quarts) buttermilk	whipped cream
½ cup sugar	

Advance Preparation: Soak the raisins in the orange juice for about 30 minutes at room temperature.

1. Mix the flour with a small amount of the buttermilk to form a smooth, thin paste. Pour the buttermilk into a large saucepan and stir in the flour mixture.

2. Add the sugar, lemon juice, lemon zest, salt, and cinnamon and stir to combine.

3. Carefully heat the buttermilk mixture until it just begins to simmer and thickens slightly. Stir in the raisins and orange juice. Cook over very low heat 2 minutes.

4. Serve hot, topped with a dollop of chilled whipped cream.

Notes: Versions of this recipe abound. The soup may be thickened with 4 ounces of ground rice instead of the flour. Eggs may be beaten into the hot soup just before serving. There is also a cold version of this soup, but the use of raw eggs is not recommended by this author.

Meat Soup

Kødsuppe

There are no set types or amounts of meats in Danish recipes for meat soup. It may be made exclusively from beef or, as in this recipe, from a combination of beef, pork, and chicken. Regardless, a proper Danish broth is very clear and should be meticulously skimmed and strained. This soup is the base for adding such goodies as forcemeat dumplings (*kødboller*, see page 24) and egg dumplings (*melboller*, see page 23). Separately cooked carrots are usually added just before serving.

---

1 chicken (about 3 pounds)

2 pounds beef or veal shanks

2 pounds country-style pork ribs

salt

4 carrots, peeled and diced

chopped parsley

dumplings (optional, see pages 23 and 24)

Advance Preparation: This broth may be made several days in advance and reheated, allowing time to make dumplings or meatballs just before serving.

1. Place the chicken, beef shanks, and pork ribs in a large stockpot. Add enough cold water to cover, about 12 cups. Add 2 teaspoons salt and bring just to a boil. Immediately lower heat and simmer over low heat until the meats fall from the bones, about 1½ hours, skimming often (see Notes).

2. While the broth is cooking, steam the diced carrots or simmer in water until tender but not soft. If adding meatballs or dumplings, they would be made at this time.

3. Remove the meats and bones and pass the broth through a cheesecloth-lined strainer. Adjust seasoning with salt.

4. Add portions of cooked carrots (and any other additions prepared) to soup bowl and ladle hot broth over. Top with chopped parsley and serve immediately.

Notes: To make a clear broth several techniques are important. Always start with cold water. Allow the soup to just come to a boil and immediately turn the heat to a low setting to barely simmer the liquid. After a minute or so, skim off the coagulated proteins from the surface, which will also help prevent boil-over accidents, and continue to skim often while the meats are simmering.

Soup Dumplings

Melboller

These little dumplings are the perfect addition to *kødsuppe* (meat soup, page 22). They are given honor by inclusion in a Danish adage meaning to embellish a story, the literal translation from the Danish being "to garnish the soup with dumplings." *("At sætte boller på suppen.")*

8 tablespoons butter	1 cup boiling water
1 cup all-purpose flour	5 eggs, at room temperature

Advance Preparation: The batter may be made one day in advance and stored in the refrigerator.

1. Melt the butter in a saucepan over low heat. Stir in the flour.

2. Beat in the boiling water, stirring constantly until it forms a smooth dough that leaves the sides of the bowl. Allow to cool several minutes.

3. Beat in the eggs, one at a time, to form a smooth paste.

4. Drop very small spoonfuls of batter into simmering salted water, being careful not to crowd the pan. Cook 2 minutes, flip the dumplings over, and cook one minute more. Remove with a slotted spoon to a tray or pan. Use as directed in soup recipe.

Notes: The eggs may be separated and the whites then beaten separately and folded into the batter.

Forcemeat Dumplings for Soup

Kødboller

The Danes have a love affair with ground meats. Finely ground meats are called forcemeat. They form the forcemeat into patties and balls, and fry them, sauté them, and simmer them in sauce. They also make small dumplings and serve them in soup. Regardless of the form or cooking method, the forcemeat is always very smooth, the result of multiple grindings of the meat, fish, or poultry.

1 pound beef chuck, ground 4 times (see Notes)

1 small onion, finely grated or puréed

3 tablespoons all-purpose flour

2 eggs

salt and pepper

Advance Preparation: Grind the beef 4 times, passing successively through a meat grinder. The mixture should be very smooth. Heat the water to cook the dumplings.

1. Mix the grated onion with the ground beef. Add the flour and stir to incorporate.

2. Beat in one egg at a time. Adjust seasoning with salt and pepper—you may pan-fry a small portion to check for correct seasoning.

3. Shape the forcemeat into marble-size balls and drop them into simmering salted water for 2 minutes. Turn them over and cook an additional 2 minutes. Use as directed in soup recipe (page 22).

Notes: If using a food processor to grind the beef, be careful not to overheat the meat as it is being processed. You can add a cube or two of ice to the work bowl for temperature control.

Fruit Soup

Sød Suppe

Fruit soups are conveniently made with sweetened fruit juices, but can also be made with fresh and dried fruits. When fruit soups are thickened, sago starch is often used. It also comes in pearls, resembling tapioca, and tapioca or cornstarch may be substituted for sago in recipes.

---

6 cups sweetened fruit juice, such as berry or cherry juice

zest of 1 lemon, cut in long strips

1 cinnamon stick

½ cup sago starch (see Notes)

soup dumplings (*melboller*) (optional, see page 23)

Advance Preparation: The soup dumplings will have to be made, if using.

1. Heat the fruit juice with the lemon zest and cinnamon stick over low heat for 5 minutes.

2. Make a thin paste of sago starch with some cold water.

3. Remove the lemon peel and cinnamon stick and whisk in the sago paste. Continue to cook over low heat until the soup has thickened and is clear.

4. Place a few soup dumplings into each bowl (if using) and ladle hot soup over. Serve immediately.

Notes: Dried plums or raisins may be plumped in hot fruit juice and added to the soup. Toasted and buttered croutons may substitute for the dumplings. Other thickeners, such as cornstarch or tapioca starch may be used. Always add a little of the paste at a time, to observe its thickening strength.

Apple Soup

Æblesuppe

Sour apples are the secret to this soup, and their tartness should not be masked by the sugar added. Crushed zwieback crisps are often placed in the bowl before serving.

---

4 large tart apples, such as Granny Smith, Cortland, or Pippin, quartered (unpeeled and uncored)

zest of 1 lemon, cut in long strips

¼ teaspoon cinnamon, or 1 cinnamon stick

sugar to taste

cornstarch stirred into water to make a thin paste

Advance Preparation: Up to one day in advance, cook the quartered apples in 8 cups water until very tender. Remove the cooked apples and pass them through a sieve or strainer. Strain and reserve the cooking liquid.

1. Heat the apple cooking liquid over low heat and stir in the strained apples. Add the lemon zest and cinnamon. Simmer 5 minutes over low heat.

2. Remove the lemon zest and add sugar to taste (do not mask the tartness of the apples).

3. Add small amounts of the cornstarch paste, allowing each portion to thicken before deciding to add more, until the soup has a creamy texture. Simmer 2 minutes. Serve hot.

Notes: Tart pears would make a delicious fruit soup. Add a few gratings of nutmeg to replace the cinnamon. Crushed biscotti or zwieback can be added to bowls before serving.

Cold Cherry Soup

Serves 6

Kirsebær Kold Skål

Hot fruit soups are usually served as the prelude to a meal. Cold fruit soups are often served as dessert, and also make an excellent palate cleanser between courses.

---

2 pounds ripe cherries, pitted (see Notes), pits reserved

2 cups sugar

1 cinnamon stick

zest of 1 lemon, cut in long strips

⅓ cup cherry liqueur, such as Peter Heering

whipped cream (optional)

Advance Preparation: Pit the cherries, reserving both the cherries and the pits (see Notes).

1. Add the pitted cherries, sugar, and 8 cups water to a stockpot. Bring to a boil, reduce the heat, and simmer 2 minutes. Remove the cherries and reserve.

2. Crush the cherry pits in a mortar or briefly pulse using a food processor. Add them to the hot liquid with the cinnamon stick, and lemon zest. Simmer 5 minutes.

3. Strain the soup and add the cherries. Allow to cool.

4. Stir in the cherry liqueur and chill thoroughly. Serve cold with a dollop of whipped cream, if desired.

Notes: To pit cherries, place them in a heavy resealable plastic bag. Tap on the cherries with a kitchen mallet. They will easily break apart, releasing the pits. Be careful not to pulverize the cherries. This technique also works well to pit olives.

Salads

Salads are served alongside meat dishes, as a first course, and quite importantly, on *Smørrebrød*, the traditional open-face sandwich buffet table. Herring salads are extremely popular, as evidenced by the variations that abound. Cold-weather vegetables, such as potatoes, cabbages, and beets, are the main ingredients for Danish salads. The dressing, tossed with the salad before serving, is often just a generous dollop of thick, rich sour cream.

Pickled Herring Salad (Hakket Sildesalat)

Anchovy Salad (Ansjossalat)

Salmon Salad (Lakssalat)

Red Cabbage Salad (Rødkålssalat)

Coleslaw (Kålsalat)

Warm Potato Salad (Varm Kartofflesalat)

Cold Potato Salad (Kold Kartoffelsalat)

Sour Cream Potato Salad (Kartoffelsalat med Sur Fløde)

Lettuce with Sour Cream (Salat med Sur Fløde)

Cucumber Salad (Agurkesalat)

Pickled Herring Salad

Hakket Sildesalat

Herring is eaten for breakfast, lunch, dinner, and as an evening snack with drinks in a variety of forms. This humble fish rises to honored status throughout Scandinavia. The best herring are said to come from Bornholm, a tiny Danish island in the Baltic nestled between Poland and Sweden. The version below is a pickled herring salad, but there are recipes that call for smoked herrings as well.

1 pound pickled herring, coarsely chopped (see Notes)	2 tablespoons sugar
3 cooked beets, peeled and diced	2 tablespoons pickling liquid from the pickled herrings
2 small tart apples, peeled, cored, and diced	⅔ cup sour cream
2 tablespoons grated onion	sliced hard-boiled eggs (optional)

Advance Preparation: This salad should be made one day in advance to develop flavor.

1. Toss the chopped herrings with the beets, apples, and grated onion. Refrigerate, covered, for 2 hours.

2. Mix the sugar and pickling liquid into the sour cream. Stir this into the fish mixture. Refrigerate at least 30 minutes before serving and up to one day.

3. Garnish with sliced eggs, if using, and serve.

Notes: Commercial pickled herring in jars works well in this dish, but homemade would be superior. In Denmark, only freshly prepared pickled herring would be used. See page 48 for a recipe.

Anchovy Salad

Ansjossalat

This is a composed salad, with the vegetables arranged around prepared anchovy paste. Scandinavian anchovies are different from those typically found in jars and cans and are not the anchovies typically found on pizza or in salad dressings. Rather they are a different fish species related to the sardine.

---

24 salt-packed anchovy fillets (see Notes)

¼ cup freshly squeezed lemon juice

1 teaspoon prepared mustard

¼ cup light oil, such as safflower or canola

freshly ground black pepper

⅓ cup coarsely chopped sweet pickles

12 ripe pitted olives, halved

2 ounces smoked salmon, cut into thin strips

12 cherry tomatoes, halved

Advance Preparation: All advance preparation may be found in the ingredient list

1. Rinse the anchovies and pat dry. Mash them with a fork to form a smooth paste.

2. Prepare the dressing by whisking the lemon juice with the mustard. Slowly whisk in the oil. Add a few grinds of pepper and reserve.

3. Compose individual salads (or one large salad) by placing the mashed anchovies in the center of the plate. Arrange the pickles, olives, smoked salmon, and cherry tomatoes around the anchovies. Drizzle dressing over the salad and serve.

Notes: Salt-packed anchovies should be sought out for this dish. They look like little whole fish, with heads and tails removed. If using oil-packed anchovies, drain well before using. Reserve some of the oil for the vinaigrette. You may want to increase the number of fillets used.

Salmon Salad

Lakssalat

Second only to herring, salmon are treasured throughout Scandinavia. Norwegian salmon are processed in Denmark and are eaten fresh, smoked, and salt cured. For this salad, fresh salmon fillet is poached.

---

12 ounces salmon fillet

vegetable stock, court bouillon, or water to poach the salmon

1 sprig dill

2 small Roma tomatoes, quartered

1 cucumber, peeled, seeded, and coarsely chopped

2 tablespoons lemon juice

1 teaspoon sugar

pinch salt

⅔ cup mayonnaise

chopped parsley

Advance Preparation: Poach the salmon in the liquid of your choice, along with the dill, until done, about 8 minutes. Allow to cool. Refrigerate until needed. Discard the poaching liquid.

1. Gently crumble the cooled salmon in a bowl. Toss in the tomatoes and cucumber.

2. Mix the lemon juice, sugar, and salt with the mayonnaise. Gently fold this dressing into the salmon mixture. Refrigerate until chilled.

3. Serve portions of salad topped with chopped parsley.

Notes: In a pinch, quality canned salmon can be used for this recipe, but the results will not be the same. Be sure to thoroughly drain the canned salmon. It may be improved by briefly blanching in vegetable stock or court bouillon.

Red Cabbage Salad

Rødkålssalat

What could be more Danish that to dress a salad with whipped cream? Look past the cholesterol to enjoy a most tasty slaw.

1 medium head red cabbage, outer leaves removed, coarsely chopped

1 Granny Smith or other tart apple, peeled, cored, and diced

1 cup diced celery stalks, from the tender interior

juice of 1 lemon

pinch salt

freshly ground pepper

2 tablespoons honey

1 cup heavy cream

Advance Preparation: All advance preparation may be found in the ingredient list.

1. Mix the chopped cabbage with the diced apple and celery. Toss with lemon juice, salt, pepper, and honey.

2. Whip the cream to firm but not stiff peaks. Fold it into the cabbage mixture. Chill thoroughly.

3. Serve on chilled plates.

Notes: The cabbage may be salted before using to remove some of the liquid. Toss the cut cabbage with 2 tablespoons coarse salt and allow to stand 10 minutes. Rinse with cold water and thoroughly drain before using.

S olvang, California was founded in 1911 as a Danish cultural community in the Santa Ynez Valley, a part of Rancho San Carlos de Jonata. A group of Midwest Danish educators wanted to establish a folk school of Danish tradition and named it "Sunny Field" (*Solvang* in Danish). The rich soil attracted farmers, soon to be followed by carpenters and artisans, establishing the largest Danish-American community in the U.S. The downtown area is exclusively of Danish architecture and the original schoolhouse still stands as a local restaurant.

Coleslaw

Kålsalat

Cabbages thrive in cool weather and store well in cold cellars, perfect for the Danish climate. The name "coleslaw" derives from the Latin *cole* for cabbage (*kål* in Danish). Two types of coleslaw are found on American plates, the creamy style based on mayonnaise, and a vinegar-based slaw as found below.

1 medium head green cabbage, outer leaves removed	1 tablespoon sugar
salt	1 teaspoon celery seed
½ cup canola oil	1 red bell pepper, seeded, finely diced
⅓ cup apple cider vinegar	salt and pepper to taste
2 tablespoons grated onion	

Advance Preparation: Quarter and core the cabbage. Coarsely shred and toss it with some salt. Allow to stand 30 minutes. Drain the liquid that is released and rinse the cabbage under cold water. Drain thoroughly.

1. Whisk the oil with the vinegar, grated onion, sugar, and celery seed.

2. Toss the cabbage with the bell pepper and add the dressing, gently mixing to combine.

3. Refrigerate 1 hour. Adjust seasoning with salt and pepper. Serve chilled.

Notes: You may skip the salting of the cabbage. If so, cut back a little on the amount of dressing added.

Warm Potato Salad

Varm Kartofflesalat

Not just picnic fare, potato salads make a tasty side dish any time, and can be found on every *Smorgåsbørd* table. This potato salad is served warm, with mayonnaise stirred in just before it goes to the table.

8 ounces thick-sliced bacon	¼ cup water
4 pounds new potatoes	¼ cup sugar
1 large onion, diced	salt and pepper to taste
½ cup cider vinegar	¾ cup mayonnaise

Advance Preparation: Sauté the bacon over low heat until crisp. Drain on paper towels, saving the bacon fat, and crumble the bacon. See Note.

1. Boil the potatoes whole and unpeeled, in sufficient water, until tender. Peel the potatoes while hot and cut into small pieces.

2. Sauté the onion in some of the reserved bacon fat until soft, but not browned.

3. Add the vinegar, water, and sugar to the sautéed onion and heat to a boil.

4. Pour the hot onion mixture over the potatoes and toss gently. Stir in the crumbled bacon.

5. Just before serving adjust seasoning with salt and pepper and stir in the mayonnaise. Serve warm.

Notes: This salad can be made in advance, less the mayonnaise, and refrigerated until needed. The potato salad is then warmed and the mayonnaise stirred in just before serving.

Cold Potato Salad

Kold Kartoffelsalat

Fresh dill is an often-used herb in Danish cuisine and is featured in this cold potato salad. Danes enjoy the flavor of curry, also making an appearance in this popular side dish to cold meats and Danish ham.

2 pounds russet potatoes	2 tablespoons minced shallots
⅔ cup mayonnaise	salt and pepper to taste
pinch curry powder	
¼ cup chopped dill (include some stems)	

Advance Preparation: All advance preparation may be found in the ingredient list.

1. Peel the potatoes and cut into pieces. Cook in sufficient water until just tender, about 10 minutes. Drain the potatoes and reserve.

2. Mix the mayonnaise with the curry powder, dill, and shallots.

3. Carefully fold this dressing into the potatoes while they are still warm. Adjust seasoning with salt and pepper.

4. Refrigerate salad until thoroughly chilled. Serve cold.

Notes: A pinch of cayenne may be added to this recipe. Celery seed may substitute for the curry powder.

Sour Cream Potato Salad

Kartoffelsalat med Sur Fløde

The Danish approach to sour cream is to add it whenever possible, and it will improve that recipe. It is certainly true for potato salad, usually dressed only with mayonnaise.

3 hard-boiled eggs, yolks separated from the whites

4 pounds russet potatoes, peeled, diced, boiled until tender, and drained

1 medium cucumber, peeled, seeded, and coarsely chopped

½ cup mayonnaise

1 tablespoon grated onion

1 teaspoon celery seed

2 cups sour cream

⅓ cup cider vinegar

salt and pepper to taste

Advance Preparation: The eggs and potatoes may be cooked well in advance of assembly.

1. Chop the cooked egg whites and add them to the potatoes. Toss in the chopped cucumber.

2. Mash the egg yolks in the mayonnaise and then stir in the grated onion and celery seed. Mix in the sour cream. Whisk in the vinegar.

3. Carefully toss the potato mixture with this dressing. Refrigerate 1 hour.

4. Adjust seasoning with salt and pepper and serve chilled or at room temperature.

Notes: A teaspoon of dry mustard can be added to the dressing. Chopped parsley may be added to the top of the salad before serving.

Lettuce with Sour Cream

Serves 4

Salat med Sur Fløde

This very-easily prepared salad is delightful in its simplicity. Use organic sour cream with live cultures to approximate the luscious sour cream used in Denmark, and any loosely leafed lettuce, including Boston or romaine.

1 cup sour cream

1 tablespoon sugar

pinch salt

1 large head leaf lettuce, washed, drained, and separated into leaves

Advance Preparation: There is no advance preparation for this dish.

1. Mix the sour cream with the sugar and salt, making sure the sugar completely dissolves. Refrigerate until thoroughly chilled.

2. Tear the lettuce leaves into bite-size pieces and gently toss with the chilled sour cream dressing. Serve on chilled salad plates.

Notes: In some regions of the country, heavy cream mixed with a small amount of vinegar and sugar is used as the dressing.

Most of us have heard of the wireless specification "Bluetooth," found in many electronic devices. Its logo is the runic letters BT. Bluetooth was actually king of Denmark, ruling from 958 to about 985. Harald Blåtand (Bluetooth) Gormsen was the son of King Gorm of Old and is most famous for his construction projects to stimulate the economy of Denmark at that time. In addition, his most lasting legacy was the building of runic stones found in Jelling, to memorialize his mother, Thyra Danneblod, and father. Bluetooth brought Christianity to Denmark, constructed the oldest bridge in Scandinavia, and built the ring forts, remnants of which still stand for visitors and Danes to admire.

Cucumber Salad

Agurkesalat

Danish cucumbers can be up to 18 inches in length and just over 1 inch in diameter. They have very few seeds and taste like other cucumbers. Any cucumber variety will do for this recipe, but be sure to cut the cucumbers paper thin. This recipe improves with age, so plan on making it several hours in advance.

---

1 cup cider vinegar

2 cups sugar

2 large unpeeled cucumbers, washed, very thinly sliced (see Notes)

¼ cup chopped parsley, including some stems

salt and pepper to taste

Advance Preparation: All advance preparation may be found in the ingredient list.

1. Heat the vinegar in a non-reactive saucepan. Add the sugar and stir to dissolve over low heat. Allow to cool.

2. Toss the cucumber slices with the parsley. Gently mix with the cooled vinegar dressing.

3. Adjust seasoning with salt and pepper. Refrigerate a minimum of 3 hours or overnight.

Notes: The cucumbers must be paper thin and are best cut using a mandolin or the feed tube of a food processor. Chopped dill may be substituted for, or mixed with, the parsley.

Fish

Denmark is surrounded by water, being a country made up of a large peninsula and islands of varying size. Fishing has always been the mainstay of the diet and of commerce. Since the Middle Ages, Scandinavia has supplied fish to Europe and England, usually preserved by smoking or salting. Surrounded by the icy North Sea and the Baltic, these rich waters furnish Denmark with a plethora of common and noble seafood. From the humble herring and cod to the heralded salmon, Danes enjoy fish simply prepared. And why not? With impeccably fresh fish caught only hours before, why would one mask these gastronomic treasures with heavy sauces and overbearing spices?

Bornholm, a small island in the Baltic, is known throughout Scandinavia to have the finest herring, and herring is enthusiastically eaten during any meal in Denmark. It is usually smoked or salted, and can be pickled or prepared fresh. Plaice is very popular and is related to flounder, sole, and halibut. Denmark is also known for its eel dishes, a delicacy that has yet to catch on in the United States. Tiny pink shrimps, no bigger than 1-inch long, are surprisingly succulent, and can be found piled high on top of buttered rustic bread as part of a *Smørrebrød* lunch. Oysters from the Limfjord are some of the finest to be had, and are treasured by Danish cooks and aficionados of this tasty bivalve. Lobsters, mussels, and other shellfish round out the offering.

Regardless of the fish or shellfish used, Danish recipes are simple to prepare, respecting the freshness of just-caught seafood. Whole fish and thick fish steaks are usually poached in water or court bouillon acidified with vinegar (instead of more traditional wine). Fresh plaice and herrings are often fried in light oil. Salmon, an esteemed fish, may be smoked or cured, as well as prepared by the techniques previously mentioned. Pickling is another popular way to enhance flavor while preserving the bounty of the sea, and pickled herring is a staple in most Danish households.

Marinated Salt Herring (Marinered Sild)

Salted Herring with Cream (Bondesild)

Poached Herrings (Kogt Sild)

Fried Herrings (Sild Rødspætter)

Pickled Herring (Neglagte Sild)

Mustard Herring (Sennepssild)

Cured Salmon (Gravlaks)

Salmon in Aspic (Lax i Gele)

Poached Salmon (Laks)

Fried Plaice or Flounder (Stegte Rødspætterfileter)

Baked Cod (Torsk På Fad)

Codfish Stew (Plukfisk)

Poached Cod (Kogt Torsk)

Codfish Balls (Torskboller)

Shrimp in Beer (Rejer i Øl)

Curried Eel (Aal i Karry)

Fish Forcemeat / Minced Fish (Fiskefars)

Fish Cakes (Fiskrouletter)

Marinered Sild

Salted herrings can be whole or filleted and must undergo a thorough soaking before use. They can be found in many specialty delicatessens. Herrings in brine are treated as salted herrings, and also must be soaked before using in any recipe.

4 salt herring fillets	1 small red onion, thinly sliced
milk to soak the fillets	2 cups white wine vinegar or cider vinegar
4 allspice berries	¼ cup water
2 large bay leaves	½ cup sugar
1 teaspoon whole peppercorns	buttered dark rye bread
1 small carrot, peeled and cut into thin rounds	

Advance Preparation: Soak the salt herring fillets in enough milk to cover for 12 to 24 hours. Drain and cut into large pieces. Discard the milk. Pack the fillets in a clean jar.

1. Mix the allspice, bay leaves, peppercorns, carrot, and onion with the vinegar in a non-reactive saucepan. Heat over a low flame 2 minutes.

2. Stir in the water and sugar and continue to cook over low heat until the sugar dissolves and the marinade is aromatic. Allow the marinade to thoroughly cool.

3. Pour the cooled marinade along with the vegetables and spices over the fish in the jar. Cover and refrigerate overnight.

4. Serve chilled, right from the jar, accompanied by a tray of buttered bread.

Notes: Water may replace the milk as the soaking liquid. The allspice berries may be crushed with the back of a knife before adding them for additional flavor. For a more interesting presentation, alternate layers of fish, carrots, and onions before adding the liquid.

Salted Herring with Cream

Serves 6

Bondesild

This recipe combines two of the most important ingredients in Danish cuisine—herring and rich dairy cream. Danish cooks like to whip cream before using in many savory dishes.

4 salt herring fillets

equal parts milk and water to soak the herring

1 cup heavy cream

2 tablespoons cider vinegar

1 tablespoon sugar

1 medium onion, grated

1 tart apple, peeled, cored, and grated

parsley or watercress to garnish

Advance Preparation: Soak the salt herrings overnight in a mixture of milk and water. Drain and reserve.

1. Whip the cream until thick and firm. Stir in the vinegar and sugar.

2. Cut the soaked herring fillets into 1-inch pieces and place them in a bowl.

3. Top the fillets with the grated onion and apple.

4. Cover this with the seasoned whipped cream. Add some chopped parsley or watercress and serve chilled.

Notes: A few sprigs of dill may be chopped and added to the whipped cream. Lemon juice may replace the vinegar.

B ornholm sits in the Baltic Sea quite far east of mainland Denmark. This tiny island is a seven-hour ferry ride from Køge or a thirty-minute flight from Copenhagen. The Danes refer to the island as the "Sunshine Island," best known for the fine herring caught nearby and smoked in smokehouses easily identified from afar by their distinctive tall, white chimneys rising majestically at the corners of the buildings. Hasle is one of Bornholm's oldest villages, and is host to its annual herring festival, one of the most popular food festivals in Denmark. The small town of Gudhjem accommodates the largest collection of smokehouses, several of which double as museums for the herring industry. Bornholm is home to several distinctive round churches (*rundkirk*) built between 1150 and 1200. That they have stood proud and undamaged for so many years is a tribute to their seven-foot-thick granite walls, meant to thwart pirate attacks.

Poached Herring

Kogt Sild

Herrings are a reasonably priced fish in Denmark. They are also very rich due to their high fat content, so a little goes a long way. Use the technique given below anytime poaching is called for when using fresh herrings.

---

4 whole fresh herrings, cleaned, heads removed

3 cups water

1 cup vinegar

1 teaspoon salt

1 tablespoon whole peppercorns

1 medium onion, quartered

boiled red skin potatoes, buttered

good quality white wine vinegar

Advance Preparation: The potatoes should be cooked in advance for this dish.

1. Place the herrings in a large, non-reactive saucepan. Add the water and vinegar and heat over a low flame.

2. Add the salt, peppercorns, and onion and bring to a boil. Immediately lower the heat to a simmer. Simmer 5 to 7 minutes, skimming often. Remove the fish and drain.

3. Serve the poached herrings with potatoes on the side. Have a bottle of good white wine vinegar on the table for seasoning.

Notes: Fillets work well for this dish. Reduce poaching time to 3 to 4 minutes.

Fried Herring

Sild Rødspætter

Fresh herrings are most often fried, and Danish cooks like to fry fish when it is not first preserved by salting, smoking, or pickling. Butter is used for frying as often as canola oil, the preferred cooking oil in Denmark.

---

8 fresh herring fillets, gently flattened with the back of a knife

flour for dredging

2 eggs

pinch salt

1 cup dry unseasoned breadcrumbs

8 tablespoons unsalted butter plus additional for frying

2 lemons, cut into wedges

---

1. Dredge the herring fillets in flour and pat off any excess flour.

2. Whisk the eggs with a little water and some salt and dredge the floured fillets in this mixture.

3. Allowing the fillets to drain for a moment and then dredge them in breadcrumbs.

4. Heat some butter in a large skillet until it foams. Add the battered herring and gently sauté on one side for 2 minutes. Turn and cook an additional 2 minutes. Reserve on a warm plate.

5. Heat the 8 tablespoons unsalted butter in a small saucepan until bubbling. Continue to cook until the butter solids begin to brown.

6. Pour some browned butter over the fried herrings. Serve with lemon wedges.

Notes: The fish can also be fried in oil. Use an oil low in saturated fat and trans fat, such as canola oil. For additional flavor add some butter to the cooking oil.

Pickled Herring

Neglagte Sild

Pickled herrings are used as appetizers, snack food, an accompaniment to the *Smorgåsbørd* table, and to make salads and Danish open sandwiches.

---

4 salt herring fillets (see Advance Preparation)

1 large sweet onion, sliced into thin rings

1 cup white vinegar mixed with 1 cup water

1 bay leaf

2 sprigs dill, chopped

Advance Preparation: Soak the herring fillets in 8 cups cold water for 4 hours. Drain and rinse the fillets.

1. Cut the herring fillets into square pieces. Alternate layers of fish and onion rings in a shallow non-reactive dish.

2. Pour the diluted vinegar over and add the bay leaf. Cover and refrigerate overnight.

3. To serve, drain the herring and discard the liquid. Toss the fish and onion rings with the chopped dill. Serve cold.

Notes: Parsley may replace the dill. Quality white wine vinegar would improve flavor. A pinch of sugar may be added to the pickling liquid.

Mustard Herring

Sennepssild

Matjes herrings are used in this dish. The Dutch invented this technique of mildly salting (brining) herrings caught before breeding season (when the fat content is highest at 15 percent), allowing enzymes to slowly break down the rich flesh.

4 *matjes* herrings, cut crosswise into 1-inch pieces

2 tablespoons prepared Dijon mustard

⅓ cup canola or other vegetable oil

½ cup light cream

1 tablespoon sugar

2 tablespoons diced pickled beets

1 tablespoon chopped chives

buttered pumpernickel rye bread

Advance Preparation: This recipe should be made at least 4 hours in advance of serving.

1. Place the herring pieces in a glass jar.

2. Whisk the mustard with the oil and cream to form an emulsion. Stir in the sugar and diced beets.

3. Pour this over the herring pieces. Top with chopped chives and cover. Refrigerate at least 4 hours or overnight. Serve with buttered rye bread.

Notes: Chopped pickles may replace the beets. One large smoked herring can replace the *matjes* herrings in this recipe. Boiled new potatoes are often served along with this dish. Toss them with some fresh dill and add curls of cold butter.

Cured Salmon

Gravlaks

This ancient method of preparing salmon is Swedish in origin. The Danes have more recently adopted this tasty preservation technique. Springtime is recommended for making this dish, as the dill will be fresh and particularly flavorful.

1 salmon fillet (about 1½ pounds)

½ cup salt

¼ cup sugar

6 peppercorns, crushed with the back of a knife

1 bunch fresh dill, coarsely chopped, stems included

Advance Preparation: This recipe must be made at least 24 hours (preferably 48 hours) before serving.

1. Lay the salmon fillet, skin-side down, on a sheet of plastic wrap.

2. Mix the salt, sugar, and peppercorns together. Rub the flesh side of the fillet thoroughly with a portion of this mixture.

3. Spread the chopped dill uniformly over the salmon. Add the remaining salt mixture and seal tightly with plastic wrap.

4. Put the wrapped salmon fillet into a large pan and place a plate on top. Add some weights to the plate (canned goods from the pantry work well) and refrigerate 24 to 48 hours.

5. To serve, remove the salmon fillet from the plastic wrap and scrape off the curing mixture and dill. Slice very thin.

Notes: This recipe works well for 2 fillets. Have the first fillet skin-side down on the plastic film. Cover with the curing ingredients and lay the second fillet flesh-side down onto it. Orient the top fillet to have its thin end over the thick end of the fillet below. For an unexpected garnish, cut the cured salmon skin into squares and grill them.

Salmon in Aspic

Lax i Gele

This recipe is an excellent way to serve salmon cold. It makes a tasty Danish-style lunch served with a refreshing cucumber salad.

---

4 4-ounce salmon steaks
½ cup cider vinegar
6 cups salted water
1 tablespoon whole peppercorns
2 tablespoons unflavored gelatin
    softened in ¼ cup cold water

1 cup hot fish broth
mayonnaise
cucumber salad (optional) (see page 40)

Advance Preparation: Prepare the fish broth, if making fresh. This dish will need to set for about 3 hours before serving. Prepare the cucumber salad, if using.

1. Place the salmon steaks in a large, non-reactive pan. Mix the vinegar with the salted water and peppercorns and pour over salmon. Gently poach the salmon for about 8 minutes.

2. Dissolve the softened gelatin in the hot fish broth.

3. Arrange the poached salmon steaks in a deep serving dish. Pour the gelatin fish broth over the salmon. Allow to cool and then refrigerate until thoroughly chilled, about 3 hours.

4. Serve with a dollop of mayonnaise and a side dish of cucumber salad, if using.

Notes: A crisp green salad can replace the cucumber salad. You can add a small sprig of dill to top each salmon steak before allowing the gelatin to set. Fresh fish broth can be made with scraps of trimmed salmon or leftover shrimp shells poached in vegetable broth.

Poached Salmon

Serves 6

Laks

There are many rivers for salmon fishing in Denmark, but the catch is small and the fish are becoming endangered. Compared to the relatively abundant and tasty herring, salmon are considered a delicacy and can be quite expensive.

1 whole salmon (about 4 pounds), cleaned

½ cup cider vinegar

2 onions, peeled and quartered

2 carrots, sliced

1 stalk celery, cut into 1-inch pieces

1 bay leaf

1 bunch fresh dill

hollandaise sauce, mustard sauce, or horseradish sauce for serving

Advance Preparation: Prepare the salmon by wrapping it in cheesecloth.

1. In a non-reactive saucepan, heat 12 cups water with the vinegar, onions, carrots, celery, bay leaf, and dill over low heat. Simmer, covered, 30 minutes. Allow this court bouillon to cool before using.

2. Place the wrapped fish in a non-reactive roasting pan. Strain the cooled court bouillon and pour it over the fish. Heat to barely a simmer and cook, covered, 7 to 8 minutes per pound.

3. Carefully remove the fish when done. Gently remove the cheesecloth. The skin should come off with the cloth. Trim the fish and place on a serving platter.

4. Serve with a sauce of your choice.

Notes: Large salmon steaks may also be prepared in this manner. Reduce the cooking time to a total of 15 minutes. For fish larger than 5 pounds, add 10 minutes to the total cooking time.

Fried Plaice or Flounder

Serves 4

Stegte Rødspættefileter

Plaice is a flatfish related to sole and flounder. Frying is a popular way to enjoy this flavorful fish. When butter is not used for frying, the preferred cooking oil is rapeseed oil, known more often by the consumer-friendly name canola (Canadian oil seed low acid), and Denmark is a producer. In 2005, Denmark banned all oils containing more than 2 percent trans fat, and canola oil easily passes this requirement.

1 cup mayonnaise

⅛ teaspoon ground cayenne pepper

2 teaspoons prepared horseradish

1 tablespoon minced capers

juice of ½ lemon

1 pound plaice or flounder fillets

flour for dredging

2 eggs, beaten with 2 tablespoons water

canola oil for frying

salt and pepper

Advance Preparation: Set up a frying area with paper towels to drain the fried fish, a pair of tongs, and sufficient oil in a skillet.

1. Mix the mayonnaise with the cayenne, horseradish, capers, and lemon juice. Allow to stand refrigerated 30 minutes or more.

2. Dredge the fish fillets in flour and pat off any excess. Dip the fillets in the beaten egg mixture and allow any excess to run off. Dredge the fillets in the flour again and coat evenly.

3. Heat the canola oil to 360 degrees F. Add the fish fillets and fry for 5 to 7 minutes, or until cooked and crispy. Do not crowd the pan. Turn the fillets halfway through cooking if the fish are not immersed in the oil.

4. Drain on paper towels. Sprinkle the fish fillets with salt and pepper and serve immediately with the prepared mayonnaise sauce.

Notes: Remoulade sauce may replace the horseradish mayonnaise. The fish may be fried in butter rather than oil. Breadcrumbs may replace the second dredging in flour.

Baked Cod

Serves 6

Torsk På Fad

Cod has been over-fished in the Baltic and regulations control harvest. There has been a flurry of work on restocking this area with juvenile fish through aqua-culture. But cod is still reasonably priced and makes its way often to the Danish dinner table.

3 tablespoons butter	salt and pepper
3 tablespoons all-purpose flour	1½ pounds fresh cod fillets
2 cups warm fish or vegetable stock	⅔ cup dry unseasoned breadcrumbs
2 egg yolks	2 tablespoons butter, melted
juice of 1 lemon	

Advance Preparation: Heat the oven to 375 degrees F.

1. Melt the 3 tablespoons butter over low heat in a saucepan. Whisk in the flour and cook over low heat 3 to 4 minutes, whisking and being careful not to brown the flour.

2. Whisk in the warm stock and heat to a boil. Lower the heat and simmer 2 minutes. Remove the pan from the heat and whisk in the egg yolks and lemon juice. Adjust seasoning with salt and pepper.

3. Place the cod fillets in a deep baking dish or casserole. Top the fillets with breadcrumbs and drizzle with the melted butter.

4. Pour the sauce over the breadcrumbs and bake at 375 degrees F for 20 minutes, or until the sauce is bubbling and the fish is flaky.

Notes: White wine can replace part (or all) of the lemon juice. Chopped fresh dill may be added to the breadcrumbs.

Codfish Stew

Plukfisk

This recipe is a tasty way to use leftovers, and is often the dish served on the day following a dinner of whole poached cod.

2 tablespoons butter	salt and pepper to taste
2 tablespoons all-purpose flour	2 cups cooked, flaked cod
1½ cups cream, heated	toast points fried in butter
½ cup thinly sliced onions	4 hard-boiled eggs, halved

Advance Preparation: All advance preparation may be found in the ingredient list.

1. Melt the butter over low heat in a saucepan. Whisk in the flour and cook over low heat for about 3 minutes while whisking. Do not allow the mixture to brown.

2. Whisk in the warm cream and heat to a boil. Lower the heat and add the onions. Cook over low heat until the onions are soft, about 5 minutes. Adjust seasoning with salt and pepper.

3. Add the cod and gently stir. Warm over very low heat 5 minutes.

4. To serve, pour the codfish stew into a shallow serving dish and arrange toast points and hard-boiled eggs around the dish. Serve immediately.

Notes: A few teaspoons of brandy or sherry can be added to the cream sauce before the onions are added.

Poached Cod

Kogt Torsk

On its surface, a poached cod recipe does not sound particularly exciting. The Danes spark enthusiasm in two ways—strictly fresh fish and myriad garnishes surrounding the poached cod.

¼ cup salt

¼ cup white wine vinegar

2 bay leaves

1 tablespoon whole peppercorns

1 small whole cod (3 to 4 pounds), cleaned, cut into thick steaks

3 tablespoons butter, melted

Garnishes:

diced pickled beets

hard-boiled eggs, whites and yolks chopped separately

grated horseradish root

chopped flat-leaf parsley

capers

Advance Preparation: All garnishes should be prepared in advance of poaching the fish.

1. In a non-reactive pan, mix 8 cups water with the salt, vinegar, bay leaves, and peppercorns and bring to a boil.

2. Add the cod steaks and allow the liquid to return to a boil. Immediately remove the pan from the heat and cover tightly. Allow to stand 10 minutes.

3. Place the poached cod steaks on a platter and drizzle with melted butter. Arrange small dishes of chopped egg, beets, and other prepared garnishes, around the platter. Serve immediately.

Notes: Whole cod may also be poached in this manner. Allow 15 minutes poaching time. Mustard sauce (see page 129) can replace the melted butter. Pickled peppers, such as pepperocini or banana peppers, would make a tasty addition to the garnishes.

Codfish Balls

Serves 4 to 6

Torskboller

Cod has been preserved by salting for many centuries and salt-cod dishes are popular throughout Europe, especially in Spain (*bacalao*), Italy (*bacalà*), and Portugal (*bacalhao*). An overnight soaking of the salt cod is a must, along with several rinses to remove the excess salt.

8 ounces salt cod	2 tablespoons butter, melted
3 cups grated raw potatoes	pinch dry mustard
1 egg	½ teaspoon pepper
1 egg yolk	oil for frying

Advance Preparation: Soak the salt cod in water overnight, refrigerated. Drain and discard the soaking liquid. Add fresh, cold water and soak an additional 1 hour. Drain and rinse several times with fresh cold water.

1. Cut the reconstituted cod into pieces. Add them along with the grated potatoes to a saucepan. Cover with water and cook over medium heat until the potatoes are just tender, about 4 minutes. Drain thoroughly.

2. Whisk the egg, egg yolk, and melted butter together.

3. Flake the cod with a fork and stir in the egg mixture. Add the dry mustard and pepper and beat until a smooth batter forms. A few pulses in a food processor make short work of this.

4. Heat the oil to 375 degrees F. Drop spoonfuls of the cod mixture into the oil and fry until golden brown, turning the codfish balls occasionally. Drain on paper towels.

Notes: These fish balls make a tasty appetizer. Serve with dipping sauces such as remoulade, horseradish sauce, tartar sauce, and/or cocktail sauce.

Shrimp in Beer

Rejer i Øl

Shrimp are usually prepared as salads or are piled high on buttered bread as part of *Smørrebrød* in Denmark. Danish shrimp are tiny and very sweet; they remain tender and juicy after cooking. Larger shrimp may be enjoyed as an appetizer, often accompanied by a refreshing Danish beer such as Tuborg or Carlsberg. In this recipe the shrimp are cooked in the beer.

---

3 12-ounce bottles strong beer, such as Carlsberg Elephant

¼ cup diced onion

1 lemon, sliced

1 bay leaf

1 sprig parsley

2 pounds raw shrimp (any size), peeled and deveined

4 tablespoons butter, melted

salt

chopped fresh dill

Advance Preparation: All advance preparation may be found in the ingredient list.

1. In a large saucepan, bring the beer with the onion, lemon, bay leaf, and parsley to a simmer. Cook over very low heat 2 minutes.

2. Add the shrimp and increase the heat. Allow the liquid to come to a boil and immediately remove the pan from the heat. Cover and allow to stand 2 minutes. Drain and let the shrimp cool slightly.

3. Place the shrimp on a serving plate and drizzle with the melted butter. Sprinkle with salt and chopped dill. Serve warm.

Notes: Any strong or dark beer will do for this recipe. A few tablespoons of beer may also be added to the melted butter before drizzling over the shrimp.

Curried Eel

Aal i Karry

To those that appreciate eel, Denmark is known for some of the finest dishes served. The quality of the eels is due, in part, to aquaculture and Danish stocking of millions of selectively bred eels annually along its coastlines.

2 small eels (about 2 pounds)	1 tablespoon curry powder
1 bunch parsley	3 tablespoons all-purpose flour
3 tablespoons butter	salt and pepper
1 medium onion, diced	cooked white rice (optional)

Advance Preparation: Clean and skin the eels. Cut them into 2-inch segments.

1. Place the eel pieces into a small pot. Add 4 cups water. Top with the parsley. Heat to a simmer and cook until tender, about 8 minutes. Remove the eels to a warm plate and strain the poaching liquid. Measure 2 cups of the liquid and reserve.

2. Melt the butter in the pot used to cook the eels. Add the onion and sauté over medium heat until the onions are clear but not browned.

3. Add the curry powder and cook one minute. Add the flour and cook 2 minutes over low heat.

4. Add the 2 cups reserved poaching liquid and bring to a boil over medium heat. Lower the heat and simmer 2 minutes. Adjust seasoning with salt and pepper.

5. Pour this sauce over the eels and serve immediately, accompanied with fluffy white rice, if using.

Notes: To add interest to this dish, use hot curry powder. The eels may be fried rather than poached and the sauce made with on-hand stock or broth.

Fish Forcemeat / Minced Fish

Serves 6

Fiskefars

In Denmark, the sign of good forcemeat is that it is as smooth as possible. This can be a tedious task by hand, as it has been done for centuries. But with some care, a food processor can make short work of it.

12 ounces fish fillets, such as pike or haddock, cut into pieces

4 tablespoons butter, softened

1 egg

1 egg yolk

2 tablespoons potato flour, or 1 tablespoon all-purpose flour and 1 tablespoon cornstarch

1 teaspoon salt

chilled cream

hollandaise sauce (optional)

Advance Preparation: Have the fish, eggs, and cream as cold as possible to avoid heat damage by the food processor.

1. Add the fish to the work bowl of a food processor. Pulse several times to coarsely chop the fish. Add the butter and pulse until the butter is uniformly distributed.

2. Add the egg and yolk and pulse to incorporate. Add the flour and salt and pulse until smooth.

3. With the processor running, slowly add enough chilled cream to make the mixture smooth but firm enough to form into patties or balls.

4. Spread the forcemeat into a buttered 2-cup mold and place this into a pan with sufficient water to come halfway up the sides of the mold. Cover the mold with foil and cook on the stove or in a 425-degree-F oven for 45 minutes to 1 hour, until the filling is set.

5. Allow to cool and serve slices with hollandaise sauce, if using.

Notes: This recipe is the basis for many fish recipes, such as fish balls (*fiskadeller*) for soup and fish patties (*fiskrouletter*): Drop spoonfuls of forcemeat into simmering boiling water or form into patties and fry in butter.

Fish Cakes

Fiskrouletter

This is quite a versatile recipe. The fish used may be leftovers, reconstituted salted fish, smoked fish, canned fish, or fresh fish prepared specifically for this recipe.

4 medium russet potatoes, peeled and cut into large pieces

¼ cup cream, warmed

3 tablespoons butter, softened

salt to taste

2 cups coarsely chopped cooked fish

1 egg

butter for frying

mustard sauce (optional, see page 129)

Advance Preparation: Cook the potatoes in salted water until just tender, about 8 minutes. Drain and mash them with the warm cream and butter. Adjust seasoning with salt. Allow to cool.

1. Toss the flaked fish with the cooled mashed potatoes. Stir in the egg. Form the mixture into patties or cakes.

2. Heat butter in a large skillet over medium heat. Add the fish cakes and sauté over low heat 3 minutes per side, being careful not to crowd the pan.

3. Serve warm with mustard sauce, if using.

Notes: Chopped fresh dill may be added to the potatoes. The fish cakes may be deep-fried in oil.

The Greek contribution to the alphabet was adding vowels. The Danes considered the list of vowels lacking and added three more—æ, ø, and å, pronounced "eh", "ew", and "aw" respectively. Their position is at the end of the standard alphabet of twenty-six characters for the sake of alphabetizing words. The Danish language is not particularly melodious and spoken Danish does not correspond closely to the written form. Occasionally only the amount of time spent lingering on a vowel differentiates spoken words. For instance, pronouncing the Danish words for "drunk" (*fuld*) and "bird" (*fugl*) differs only by the amount of time articulating the vowel.

Meats

Denmark is the world's largest pork exporter, accounting for almost 25 percent of the world market. It is no surprise that Danes eat more pork per capita than any other country. Its hams are especially favored. Unlike the dry-cured hams of Italy and Spain, Danish hams are wet-cured and canned. Beef is of high quality and prevalent, especially with such a large dairy industry, and Denmark has plentiful land for grazing. Lamb is well-liked and Danes have a taste for game, reindeer (venison), and rabbit in particular.

Roasting is the most common way to cook all cuts of pork and grinding is a traditional way of preparing most meats, forming meatballs, pâtés, and dumplings. Apples and dried fruits accompany many meat recipes, along with cabbage and potatoes, not surprising for these winter-friendly foods. Hearty stews and braised meats on the menu dispel the chill of a long wintry day.

Pork and Cabbage (Flæsk og Kål)

Roast Pork (Flæskesteg)

Pork Sausages (Medisterpølse)

Blood Sausage (Blod Pølse)

Fried Pork Belly with Apples (Æbleflæsk)

Glazed Smoked Pork Loin (Glaseret Hamburgerryg)

Pork Roast with Sauerkraut in Beer (Skinke og Surkål med Øl)

Roast Spare Ribs with Apples and Prunes (Ribbensteg med Æbler og Svesker)

Danish Ham with Madeira Sauce (Kogt Skinke med Madeira)

Bacon and Potatoes (Braendende Kaerlighed)

Danish Meatloaf (Kødrand)

Whole Stuffed Cabbage (Fyldt Hvidkålshoved)

Meatballs with Sour Cream (Frikadeller i Sur Fløde)

Meatballs in Celery Sauce (Kodboller i Selleri)

Minced Beefsteak with Onions (Hakkebøf med Løg)

Stewed Beef (Bankekød)

Beef Hash (Biksemad)

Sailor's Stew—Lobscouse (Skipper Labskovs)

Danish Stew with Herbed Dumplings (Stuvet Oksekød)

Rolled Beef (Rullepølse)

Cabbage Rolls (Hvidkålrouletter)

Lamb and Cabbage (Får i Kål)

Pickled Lamb (Sprængt Lam)

Lamb and Asparagus (Lam i Asparges)

Roast Reindeer or Venison (Rensdyrssteg eller Rådyr)

Liver Pâté (Leverpostej)

Head Cheese (Sylte)

Creamed Sweetbreads (Brisselstuvning)

Roast Marinated Rabbit (Marineret Stegt Hare)

Pork and Cabbage

Flæsk og Kål

The pork originally called for in this recipe is "slightly salted pork," popular in Scandinavia and Germany. It is like bacon in that it comes from the pork belly, but it is not smoked; rather it is lightly salted. Salt pork in America is cut from the belly but is much too salty for this recipe. Fresh pork belly is called for in this version.

---

1 (2- to 3-pound) head green cabbage, rinsed, cored, and sliced

2 pounds fresh pork belly or fatty pork shoulder, cut into ½ -inch-thick strips

½ teaspoon caraway seeds

1 tablespoon peppercorns

2 tablespoons cold butter

Advance Preparation: All advance preparation may be found in the ingredient list.

1. Add half of the sliced cabbage to a heavy pot. Layer the sliced pork over and cover the pork with the remaining cabbage.

2. Toss in the caraway seeds and peppercorns and cover tightly. Cook over very low heat for 2 to 3 hours. The pork should be tender and the cabbage browned.

3. Serve the cabbage warm in a separate bowl topped with cold butter.

Notes: No water is added to the pot when cooking. The liquid released from the cabbage and pork becomes the cooking liquid. A very low heat is required to not burn the cabbage, and the pot used should have a heavy bottom.

Roast Pork

Flæskesteg

If you love falling-off-the-bone tender pork, this recipe is for you. As is done with good American barbecue, the cooking technique is "low and slow," using low heat and long cooking times.

4- to 5-pound shoulder of pork
 or fresh leg of pork, bone-in
 (preferably with rind left on)

whole cloves

peppercorns

2 tablespoons salt

1 tablespoon onion powder

cooked red cabbage (optional, see
 page 118)

cooked new potatoes sautéed in
 butter and sugar (optional, see
 page 112)

Advance Preparation: Make 1-inch-deep slits in the surface of the pork, spacing them 2 inches apart. Place cloves and peppercorns in these slits.

1. Mix the salt with the onion powder and rub on the pork, covering all of the surfaces.

2. Place the pork in a roasting pan and put in a cold oven. Turn the heat to 225 degrees F and cook for 5 to 6 hours, until the meat is very tender.

3. Remove the cloves and peppercorns before serving. Serve warm with cabbage and potatoes, if using.

Notes: Do not heat the oven in advance. For best results, the roast should be placed in a cold oven that slowly reaches 225 degrees F and is held at that temperature for at least 5 hours.

T o be the world's largest exporter of pork products, a country has to house quite a large number of pigs. In Denmark pigs outnumber residents by a factor of almost five to one (5.4 million people compared to 24 million pigs). That generates a lot of porcine waste, which must be stored and processed somewhere. The problem is that wherever it is stored and processed the smell comes along. Environmental groups such as NOAH are campaigning against these storage facilities, as are neighborhoods being affected by the odor. Claiming it is bad for tourism, pamphlets are handed out against the industry as a whole. Since the economy of Denmark relies on pigs and pork, the farmers who raise them consider this heresy.

Pork Sausages

**Makes 4
dozen sausages**

Medisterpølse

As with forcemeats, Danish cooks like a very smooth texture to their sausages, and achieve it by multiple grindings of the meat. These sausages are sometimes preserved by pickling. They are simmered in water and then placed into a crock with the cooking liquid, vinegar, and salt. The crock is then topped with a layer of lard or other dense fat.

5 pounds boneless pork shoulder, cut into cubes to fit a grinder	salt to taste
1 onion, peeled and cut into pieces	prepared sausage casings (see Notes)
1 teaspoon ground cardamom	stock or broth (pork, chicken, or vegetable)
2 teaspoons freshly ground pepper	butter
½ teaspoon ground allspice	

Advance Preparation: Grind the meat 4 times in a meat grinder. If using a food processor, make sure that the blade is sharp and the meat is semi-frozen. Carefully pulse to a very smooth texture.

1. Pass the onion through the meat grinder and mix it into the ground pork. Stir in the cardamom, pepper, and allspice.

2. Add some salt and sample the level of seasoning by frying a small patty of the meat mixture in a skillet. Adjust seasoning as needed.

3. Loosely stuff the sausage casings with the pork mixture and twist into links.

4. To cook the sausages, add the amount you want to serve to a saucepan and cover with stock or broth. Simmer 5 minutes.

5. Remove the sausages from the pan and brown in a skillet with some butter, turning occasionally. Serve warm.

Notes: The sausage casings usually come packed in salt and will have to be thoroughly rinsed, inside and out. After rinsing off and separating the casings, place one end of each over a water spigot in a sink, and carefully run water through. A sauce can be made from the cooking liquid thickened by a roux, with prepared horseradish added for flavor.

Blood Sausage

Blod Pølse

In Denmark a cloth casing is usually hand-sewn to make this sausage. In this recipe the sausage mixture is baked in a loaf pan in a water bath. It is sliced cold for *Smørrebrød* or the slices can be pan-fried in butter for a supper dish.

---

4 cups pig's blood (see Notes)
1 pound ground pork
12 ounces pork fat, finely chopped
6 tart apples, peeled, cored, and grated
2½ cups all-purpose flour

1 teaspoon baking soda
⅓ cup sugar
1 tablespoon salt
1 teaspoon freshly ground pepper

Advance Preparation: Heat the oven to 350 degrees F.

1. Mix the pig's blood with the ground pork, pork fat, and grated apples.

2. Mix 2 cups of the flour with the baking soda, sugar, salt, and pepper.

3. Combine the pork mixture with the flour mixture. This sausage mixture should be smooth and uniform. The consistency should be very thick but pourable. If too thick, add some water; if too thin, add more of the flour.

4. Pour the mixture into 2 loaf pans and place them into larger shallow pans. Add enough water to come halfway up the sides of the pans. Bake, covered with foil, at 350 degrees F until set, about 1 hour.

5. Allow to cool to room temperature. Refrigerate 3 hours before slicing.

Notes: To cook this sausage the traditional way simmer it in a cloth casing. To make a cloth casing cut white cotton cloth into a 10-inch x 5-inch rectangle. Fold in half lengthwise and stitch along the small end and up the side, forming an open cylinder. Fill with the sausage mixture and tie the open end closed. Poach the sausage in salted water for about 1 hour.

Pigs' blood can be found in Asian markets and some specialty butcher shops can order it for you.

A relatively new dining trend in America is the food trailer, but the Danes have been enjoying a tasty meal from a trailer for almost a century. The sausage wagon, called a *pølsevogn*, has been serving sausages (*pølse*) of many varieties from these carts since 1911. These wagons range from simple carts that can be moved by a bicycle or modest scooter, to larger units in semi-permanent locations. They all offer Denmark's most popular sausage, a foot long, thin red hot dog (*røde pølser*) meant to be eaten out of hand, with dipping sauces and a bun on the side to accompany. When served in a slit bun it is called a "hot dog." There are over 130 sausage wagons in Copenhagen alone, serving about 135 million *røde pølse* every year.

Fried Pork Belly with Apples

Æbleflæsk

Pork belly is the cut from which American bacon is made. Fresh pork belly has not been smoked or cured, but can be cooked in the same manner as bacon, cut into strips and pan-fried.

---

1 pound thick-sliced fresh pork belly   3 tablespoons sugar

4 tart apples

Advance Preparation: There is no advance preparation for this dish.

1. In a large skillet, fry the slices of pork over medium-low heat until crisp, pouring off and reserving the excess fat as it accumulates.

2. Core the apples, but do not peel them. Cut them into thick rings. Toss the apple slices with the sugar.

3. Fry the apple slices in some of the reserved pork fat in the same pan as the pork over medium heat, turning occasionally, until the apples are golden brown and caramelized.

4. Arrange the pork slices on a serving platter alternating with apple rings and serve immediately.

Notes: Fresh pork belly can be found in most Asian markets, as it is quite popular in Korean and Chinese dishes. Mildly cured salt pork may replace the pork belly in this recipe.

Glazed Smoked Pork Loin

Glaseret Hamburgerryg

This dish is commonly eaten by Danes on New Years Eve.

3- to 4-pound fresh smoked pork loin

1 cup red wine

2 sprigs fresh dill, bruised with the back of a knife

1 tablespoon whole peppercorns

1 bay leaf

¼ cup coarse-grain mustard

¼ cup brown sugar

pieces of cold butter

Advance Preparation: Place the pork loin in a resealable plastic bag along with the wine, dill, peppercorns, and bay leaf. Expel most of the air and allow the pork to marinate in the refrigerator at least 4 hours or up to overnight.

1. Allow the meat to come to room temperature in the marinade. Transfer the pork loin to a small roasting pan and cover with a foil tent.

2. Roast the pork loin at 400 degrees F for 45 minutes, or until the center of the roast registers 160 degrees F.

3. Mix the mustard with the brown sugar and spread over the pork. Top with pieces of cold butter and place the roast back in the oven to form a glaze, about 5 minutes. Allow to rest 10 minutes before slicing.

Notes: A pork loin that has not been smoked may be used. Add a pinch of smoked paprika to the mustard glaze, if available.

Pork Roast with Sauerkraut in Beer

Skinke og Surkål med Øl

The Jutland peninsula of Denmark borders northern Germany and is the inspiration for this Germanic-style dish. The ingredients needed represent two of Denmark's most respected products—succulent pork and crisp refreshing beer.

---

2 pounds sauerkraut, drained and rinsed

1 tablespoon whole peppercorns

1 teaspoon caraway seeds

6 cups Pilsner-style beer

3- to 4-pound pork rib roast

Advance Preparation: Place the sauerkraut, peppercorns, caraway seeds, and beer in a non-reactive saucepan. Cook over very low heat, partially covered, 1 hour. Heat the oven to 375 degrees F.

1. Brown the pork roast in a heavy roasting pan on all sides. Add the cooked sauerkraut and any remaining cooking liquid around the roast. Add some additional beer if no liquid remains.

2. Loosely cover the pan with foil and place in the heated oven. Roast for 2 hours, or until the pork is very tender.

3. Remove the meat from the bone while still warm and serve on a platter surrounded by the sauerkraut.

Notes: Grated fresh horseradish is usually served as an accompaniment. Beet salad also complements this dish.

Roast Spare Ribs with Apples and Prunes

Serves 4

Ribbensteg med Æbler og Svesker

Pork goes so well with fruit and the Danish way is "with Apples and Prunes." The spare ribs are stuffed by breaking all of the ribs of the rack in the middle, so the rack may be folded to contain a stuffing.

---

6 ounces dried plums (prunes)

3 tart apples, peeled, cored, and diced

1 teaspoon pepper

1 rack pork spare ribs, about 3 pounds, ribs broken in the middle (see Notes)

salt and pepper

Advance Preparation: Soak the prunes in warm water for 1 hour. The prunes may be soaked in apple juice or brandy for added flavor. Heat the oven to 375 degrees F.

1. Drain the prunes and coarsely chop them. Add the diced apples and pepper and mix thoroughly.

2. Season the ribs with salt and pepper. Place the apple mixture along one meaty side of the rack and fold over the other side. This will leave the bone-side of the rack out, with the meat inside, filled with the fruit mixture. Loosely tie the rack closed with kitchen string and place in a roasting pan. Pour in just enough water to cover the bottom of the pan.

3. Roast for 1½ hours, or until the meat is tender and pulling away from the bones. Serve with pan juices.

Notes: Have the butcher in the supermarket break the bones down the center of a rack of ribs you select. To do this at home, use a heavy cleaver to break each bone one at a time. If the bones are broken in several places, the ribs can be rolled to contain the stuffing, jellyroll fashion.

Danish Ham with Madeira Sauce

Kogt Skinke med Madeira

The most identifiable Danish food product worldwide could be the Danish ham. It is of superior quality and quite versatile. Danish hams are wet cured by soaking in brine, rather than dry cured where a dry rub is applied and the ham is left to cure in the air.

---

1 2-pound canned ham, preferably Danish

¼ cup sugar

¼ cup brown sugar

1 teaspoon prepared mustard

2 tablespoons plus ½ cup Madeira wine

4 tablespoons butter

4 tablespoons all-purpose flour

2 tablespoons grated onion

2 cups warm beef, pork, or chicken stock

salt and pepper to taste

Advance Preparation: Remove the ham from the can and scrape off the gelatin on the surface. Pat dry and allow to air dry 15 minutes. Heat the oven to 325 degrees F.

1. Place the ham in a small roasting pan. Mix both sugars with the mustard and 2 tablespoons wine. Spread this over the ham. Bake 30 minutes.

2. Melt the butter over low heat. Whisk in the flour and cook the roux for 3 minutes over low heat. Do not allow the flour to brown.

3. Stir in the grated onion and cook 1 minute. Whisk in the warm stock and slowly bring to a boil. Lower the heat and simmer 2 minutes.

4. Stir in the ½ cup Madeira and cook an additional 3 to 4 minutes. Adjust seasoning with salt and pepper.

5. Serve slices of ham with Madeira sauce ladled over.

Notes: Raisins plumped in warm Madeira make a tasty addition to the sauce. This raisin-Madeira sauce also makes an excellent accompaniment to cooked tongue.

Bacon and Potatoes

Braendende Kaerlighed

Unlike American-style bacon, which is cut from the belly and is often called streaky or fatty bacon elsewhere, Danish bacon comes from meatier and less fatty center cuts of pork. This recipe is typical Danish country fare.

2 large russet potatoes, peeled and cubed	chopped parsley
4 tablespoons butter	1 pound Canadian-style bacon (see Notes), thickly sliced
⅓ cup cream, scalded	beet salad (optional, see page 115)
salt and pepper to taste	

Advance Preparation: All advance preparation may be found in the ingredient list.

1. Boil the potatoes in sufficient water until tender, about 8 minutes.
2. Drain the potatoes and mash them with the butter. Beat in the hot cream until fluffy and smooth. Adjust seasoning with salt and pepper. Reserve keeping warm.
3. Fry the bacon slices over medium heat until crisp.
4. Pile the mashed potatoes high in the center of a warm platter and surround with bacon slices. Top the potatoes with chopped parsley and serve beet salad on the side, if desired.

Notes: Look for Danish canned smoked pork loin for a more traditional cut of pork. It can usually be found where the Danish canned hams are sold.

Danish Meatloaf

Kødrand

Forcemeat is an art form in Denmark and the key is proper texture. The meat must be ground several times and then beaten to an ethereal consistency. A considerable amount of liquid is worked into the ground meat, adding to its lightness.

8 ounces veal or lean beef, ground twice	1 egg
8 ounces pork, ground twice	2 cups milk, scalded and then cooled
½ cup chopped onions	salt and pepper to taste
¼ cup all-purpose flour	

Advance Preparation: Heat the oven to 350 degrees F.

1. Mix the veal, pork, and chopped onion together. Pass through a meat grinder or pulse in a food processor to form a smooth paste.

2. Stir in the flour and egg and slowly beat in the cooled scalded milk in a steady, slow stream. Add salt and pepper to taste—fry a portion of the mix in a small skillet to check for seasoning.

3. Place the meat mixture in a buttered loaf pan or ring mold. Place this in a pan and add water to come halfway up the sides.

4. Place in the heated oven and bake for 45 minutes or until firm to the touch in the center.

5. Allow the meatloaf to cool for 10 minutes before slicing.

Notes: This meatloaf is excellent served cold for *Smørrebrød* or sandwiches. When served warm, béchamel sauce and melted butter are traditional accompaniments.

Whole Stuffed Cabbage

Serves 6

Fyldt Hvidkålshoved

When it comes to cabbage, the Danes know their vegetable. A variety known to gardeners worldwide for producing tight compact heads with inner white leaves is the "Copenhagen Market Cabbage," first exported from Denmark in 1909. Another commercially popular variety is the "Danish Ballhead Cabbage."

12 ounces lean ground beef	¼ cup all-purpose flour
8 ounces lean ground pork	2 egg whites, beaten to a froth
½ cup grated onion	1 cup sparkling water
½ tablespoon salt	1 head (4 to 5 pounds) cabbage
¼ teaspoon ground allspice	melted butter (optional)

Advance Preparation: All advance preparation may be found in the ingredient list.

1. Mix the ground beef, ground pork, and grated onion. Pass this through a meat grinder or pulse briefly in a food processor.

2. Mix the salt, allspice, and flour and stir into the meat mixture. Beat in the egg whites and the sparkling water, a little at a time, until the forcemeat is light in texture.

3. Trim the stem end of the cabbage as a level base to rest on. Cut the top of the round end off to form a lid. Carefully hollow out the cabbage, leaving the sides about 1-inch thick. Reserve any removed cabbage for another use.

4. Bring a large pot of water to a boil. Fill the hollowed cabbage with the forcemeat and place the top on the cabbage. Wrap in cheesecloth and tie with kitchen string.

5. Carefully place the wrapped cabbage into the boiling water to cover. Lower the heat to a simmer and cook, partially covered, 1½ hours. When done, place the cabbage in a colander to thoroughly drain.

6. Unwrap the cabbage, remove the top, and slice into wedges to serve. If using, serve with melted butter on the side.

Notes: The cooking liquid makes an excellent stock for a sauce. Make a roux from equal parts flour and butter and add the cooking liquid. Use 1 tablespoon each of flour and butter for each cup of liquid to make a thin sauce. Adjust seasoning with salt and pepper.

Meatballs with Sour Cream

Frikadeller i Sur Fløde

When fried, Danish meatballs are called *frikadeller*, when poached they are called *medboller*. A delightful twist on a basic meatball recipe is the addition of rye breadcrumbs, giving a decidedly Scandinavian tone to this recipe.

---

2 pounds boneless beef chuck, cubed

1½ cups rye breadcrumbs (see Notes)

2½ cups whipping cream

salt and pepper to taste

flour for dredging

8 tablespoons butter

1 cup sour cream

½ cup dry red wine

dark rye bread

Advance Preparation: Grind the beef twice using a meat grinder. If using a food processor, have the meat semi-frozen before pulsing.

1. Mix the ground beef with the breadcrumbs until uniform. Beat in 2 cups of the cream, a little at a time. (Reserve the remaining ½ cup cream for the sauce.)

2. Add salt and pepper to taste—sauté a small portion of the mixture to check for seasoning. Form into small meatballs and dredge them in flour, patting off any excess.

3. Melt the butter in a large skillet and sauté the meatballs over medium heat for 3 to 4 minutes, or until the meatballs are browned and just cooked through.

4. Add the remaining ½ cup cream and the sour cream to the pan. Stir to combine with the butter and pan juices. Simmer over low heat for 2 minutes. Stir in the wine and simmer 1 minute.

5. Serve warm accompanied by thick slices of dark rye bread.

Notes: To make rye breadcrumbs, leave several slices of rye bread out overnight to dry slightly. Add them to a food processor and pulse to form coarse crumbs. The rye crumbs can be used as is or spread out on a sheet pan to dry completely for storage.

Meatballs in Celery Sauce

Kodboller i Selleri

Celeriac, or celery root, is a type of celery developed for its large root, rather than the expected stalks. Important for Denmark's climate, celery root stores well for up to 6 months under cool conditions.

1 large celery root, peeled and cut into 1-inch cubes
1 pound lean ground beef
½ cup diced onion
1 egg

pinch ground allspice
salt and pepper to taste
2 tablespoons butter
2 tablespoons all-purpose flour

Advance Preparation: Simmer the celery root in 4 cups water until tender, about 10 minutes. Strain and reserve the cooking liquid and celery separately. This can be done well in advance.

1. Mix the ground beef with the diced onion. Pass this through a meat grinder or pulse in a food processor until evenly distributed.

2. Stir in the egg and allspice. Add some salt and pepper and slowly beat in 1 cup water until the mixture is light and smooth.

3. Heat the reserved cooking liquid from the celery root to a simmer. Drop in one small piece of the forcemeat and when cooked check for seasoning. Adjust as necessary.

4. Form the forcemeat into 1-inch balls and drop them into the simmering liquid. Cook until done, about 5 minutes. Strain and measure 3 cups of the cooking liquid, adding some water if needed.

5. Melt the butter in a saucepan over low heat. Add the flour and cook the roux over low heat 3 minutes. Do not brown the flour. Whisk in the 3 cups cooking liquid and heat to a simmer.

6. Add the reserved celery root and meatballs. Cook over low heat 5 minutes. Adjust seasoning with salt and pepper. Serve warm.

Notes: Half of the ground beef may be replaced with ground pork. Sage or cloves may replace the allspice.

Minced Beefsteak with Onions

Hakkebøf med Løg

Unlike forcemeat, which is ground several times to insure a silky texture, minced or chopped beef has been ground only once. Its texture is coarse by Danish standards and is similar to ground beef in America.

1½ pounds lean ground beef (see Notes)	1 large onion, peeled and thinly sliced
salt and pepper	1 tablespoon all-purpose flour
butter for frying	

Advance Preparation: All advance preparation may be found in the ingredient list.

1. Form the ground beef into 4 large patties. Season with salt and pepper.

2. Add some butter to a large skillet and cook the beefsteaks medium rare, 3 to 4 minutes per side. Reserve the beefsteaks on a warm platter.

3. Fry the onion slices in the same pan, adding more butter as needed. Cook until golden brown. Top the beefsteaks with the fried onions.

4. Add the flour to the skillet and stir over low heat, scraping the bottom of the pan. Add about 1 cup of water and bring to a boil over medium heat. Lower the heat and simmer 2 minutes.

5. Adjust seasoning with salt and pepper and pour the sauce over the beefsteaks and onions. Serve immediately.

Notes: The beef may be chopped by hand for a more authentic texture. Cut slices from a roast and use a large kitchen knife to chop each slice. Two knives, one in each hand, makes shorter work of the task.

Stewed Beef

Bankekød

Danish beef is of the highest quality. Production is small compared to pork, but the land is rich and the cattle are well fed. This simple recipe relies on flavorful beef, with few herbs or spices to interfere.

4 8-ounce slices boneless round steak	2 medium onions, peeled and thinly sliced
flour for dredging	2 bay leaves
butter for frying	salt and pepper

Advance Preparation: All advance preparation may be found in the ingredient list.

1. Dredge the beef in flour, shaking off the excess.

2. Heat some butter in a heavy skillet and fry the beef slices over medium-high heat, browning both sides well. Remove the beef and add some more butter.

3. Lower the heat and sauté the onions until golden brown, about 5 minutes. Return the beef to the skillet and add enough water to cover the beef.

4. Add the bay leaves, cover the skillet and simmer over low heat 1½ hours, adding water as necessary.

5. Adjust seasoning with salt and pepper. Serve right from the skillet.

Notes: Mashed potatoes are the traditional accompaniment to this dish. Be sure to use rich cream and ample butter, just as the Danes would do.

Beef Hash

Biksemad

What better way to use leftover roast than in a tasty, crisp-fried hash. To serve, a poached or fried egg tops each portion.

2 cups chopped cooked beef, from leftovers such as pot roast

1 large onion, grated

2 russet potatoes, peeled and coarsely grated

pinch ground cloves

salt and pepper to taste

butter or pan drippings

1 bay leaf

4 eggs

Advance Preparation: All advance preparation may be found in the ingredient list.

1. Mix the chopped beef with the grated onion and potatoes. Add the ground cloves and salt and pepper to taste.

2. Heat some butter or drippings (or a mixture of both) in a heavy 10-inch skillet. Spread the hash mixture evenly across the bottom of the pan.

3. Cook over medium heat 2 minutes. Carefully flip the hash over and lower the heat. Add a few tablespoons of water and the bay leaf and cook slowly, partially covered, 30 minutes, until crisp and golden.

4. Poach the eggs in acidulated water or fry them in butter or bacon fat.

5. Remove the bay leaf and serve portions of hash topped with a cooked egg.

Notes: Allspice may replace the cloves. Leftover corned beef works particularly well in this recipe.

Sailor's Stew—Lobscouse

Skipper Labskovs

Lobscouse is a stew traditionally eaten by sailors of northern Europe. It is popular in England where it is called "scouse." Scandinavians use this recipe to clean out their refrigerator after a weekend of cooking.

1 large onion, peeled and thinly sliced	1 tablespoon whole allspice berries
butter	1 tablespoon whole peppercorns
1 pound leftover cooked beef, such as pot roast or brisket (see Notes)	1 bay leaf
	beef stock to cover
2 cups diced, peeled potatoes	salt and pepper to taste
	cold butter

Advance Preparation: All advance preparation may be found in the ingredient list.

1. Sauté the sliced onion in butter until golden brown. Add the beef, potatoes, allspice, peppercorns, and bay leaf.

2. Add enough beef stock to cover the mixture and simmer, uncovered, 30 minutes, or until the potatoes and meat are very tender and the liquid has been absorbed.

3. Stir the cooked mixture well and season with salt and pepper.

4. Serve hot, topped with a piece of cold butter.

Notes: Raw beef may also be used in this dish. Use 1¼ pounds of cubed lean beef and extend cooking time to 45 minutes.

Danish Stew with Herbed Dumplings

Stuvet Oksekød

This is a very old recipe and it contains a delightful surprise. The dumplings are enhanced with a fairly liberal amount of herbs for a Danish recipe.

Stew:
2 pounds boneless beef round steak, cut into cubes
2 tablespoons cider vinegar
3 tablespoons butter plus additional for frying
2 medium onions, diced
3 tablespoons all-purpose flour
2 cups warm beef broth, or more as needed
salt and pepper

Dumplings:
2 cups all-purpose flour
1 teaspoon baking powder
½ teaspoon salt
3 tablespoons chilled butter
2 tablespoons cold water
2 tablespoons minced parsley
2 tablespoons minced fresh dill

Advance Preparation: All advance preparation may be found in the ingredient list.

1. Sprinkle the beef cubes with the vinegar. Allow to stand 5 minutes.

2. Heat some butter in a large, heavy skillet. Sauté the beef over medium-high heat to brown on all sides. Remove the browned beef and add a little more butter to the pan.

3. Add the onions and sauté until golden and soft.

4. Melt the 3 tablespoons of butter in the cooked onions and add the 3 tablespoons flour. Cook over low heat 3 minutes, stirring occasionally.

5. Add the warm beef broth and stir to combine. Bring to a boil over medium heat. Lower the heat and simmer 2 minutes. Adjust seasoning with salt and pepper.

6. Add the browned beef and cook over low heat, covered, 1½ hours, adding more beef stock as needed.

7. Meanwhile make the dumplings: Sift flour with the baking powder and salt. Cut cold butter into the flour with a pastry knife, as for pie dough. Add the water and herbs and mix quickly to form a ball. Roll portions of dough into small balls. Drop them into the stew and cook over low heat an additional 30 minutes.

8. Arrange the meat on a servng platter with the dumplings surrounding. Drizzle sauce over and serve warm.

Notes: Fresh marjoram can replace the dill. Add 1 cup sliced carrots to the stew when cooking the dumplings, if desired. Sprinkle fresh herbs over the platter for an added flavor boost.

Rolled Beef

Rullepølse

The Danish love for marinated foods also includes beef recipes. The roll of beef is first marinated for several days before cooking and is then pressed under heavy weight to cool. Slices make an excellent sandwich, perfect for *Smørrebrød*.

1½-pound flank or skirt steak

2 tablespoons minced parsley

2 tablespoons finely diced onion

1 tablespoon plus 1 cup salt

1 teaspoon ground pepper

¼ teaspoon ground allspice

¼ teaspoon ground cloves

½ cup sugar

Advance Preparation: The meat should marinate for at least 3 days before cooking.

1. Pound the steak to form a large rectangular surface.

2. Mix together the parsley, diced onion, 1 tablespoon salt, pepper, allspice, and cloves. Spread this mixture evenly across the surface of the meat.

3. Roll the meat jellyroll-fashion and tie securely with kitchen twine.

4. Mix the 1 cup salt and the sugar with 8 cups boiling water. Stir to combine and then cool completely. Add the rolled beef and completely cover with the liquid and refrigerate 3 to 5 days.

5. Drain and rinse the beef roll. Place into a pot and cover with cold water. Slowly bring the liquid to a boil. Lower the heat to a simmer and cook, partially covered, 2½ hours, adding water as needed.

6. When done remove the beef roll to a platter and place some weights on top. Refrigerate 3 hours under the weights. To serve, slice thin for sandwiches.

Notes: The marinated beef roll may be cooked in beef stock. Other herbs, such as marjoram or dill, may be added to the filling.

Cabbage Rolls

Serves 4 to 6

Hvidkålrouletter

Stuffing vegetable leaves has been a preparation method for many years. Grape leaves have been stuffed with vegetables, rice, and ground meats for centuries. Due to the climate of Scandinavia and Eastern Europe, cold-weather-friendly cabbage leaves are a more practical leaf wrapper for this traditional preparation.

1 large head green cabbage, cored	⅔ cup dry unseasoned breadcrumbs
12 ounces ground beef	1 cup milk
12 ounces ground pork	salt and pepper to taste
1 medium onion, grated	butter for frying
1 egg	browned butter

Advance Preparation: Place the whole cabbage in a large pot of boiling water. Blanch for 1 minute, remove the cabbage, and carefully peel off as many leaves as can be easily removed. Repeat the process until all of the large and medium-size leaves are removed whole.

1. Mix the ground beef, ground pork, grated onion, egg, and breadcrumbs. Slowly beat in the milk to form a smooth, light filling.

2. Place 2 tablespoons of filling into the center of a blanched cabbage leaf. Roll up, folding the sides in as you roll. Secure with a toothpick. Repeat until all the rolls have been formed.

3. Heat some butter in a large skillet and brown the cabbage rolls, in batches, on all sides.

4. Pour in water to just cover the cabbage rolls and simmer, partially covered, for 30 minutes.

5. Remove the cabbage rolls to a warm platter and drizzle with browned butter. Serve immediately.

Notes: The liquid remaining after cooking the cabbage rolls may be thickened and used as a sauce. Cooked rice (1 cup) may be added to the meat mixture. Any forcemeat recipe will do for the filling.

Lamb and Cabbage

Serves 6

Får i Kål

Danish meats are considered among the best in Europe, and most think of their superior pork products. But Danish lamb may be Denmark's best kept secret, and succulent lamb chops find their way onto many backyard grills during the short Danish summer. Other cuts are eaten year round.

---

2 to 3 pounds boneless lamb shoulder or leg, cut into uniform cubes

butter for browning

1 small onion, thinly sliced

1 small green cabbage, outer leaves discarded, cored, separated into leaves

2 tablespoons whole peppercorns

1 teaspoon salt

1 bay leaf

salt to taste

chopped parsley

buttered dark rye bread

Advance Preparation: All advance preparation may be found in the ingredient list.

1. In a large skillet, brown the lamb cubes in butter over medium heat in a large skillet. Remove the lamb and add the onion slices. Sauté until golden, about 4 minutes. Remove the onions and toss them with the lamb.

2. In a large casserole dish, alternate layers of cabbage leaves with lamb, adding peppercorns and salt to each layer. Toss in the bay leaf and cover the ingredients with cold water.

3. Heat the liquid to a boil and then lower the heat to a simmer. Cover and cook 1½ hours.

4. When done, adjust seasoning with salt and sprinkle with chopped parsley. Serve with buttered rye bread.

Notes: The juices in the casserole after cooking may be thickened with a paste of flour and water. Be sure to simmer the sauce for a few minutes to remove any raw flour taste.

Pickled Lamb

Sprængt Lam

Pickling not only allows for extended storage and preservation, but the textural changes and flavors that develop are preferred by the Danish palate.

---

1 cup salt

½ cup sugar

1 sprig dill, chopped

3-pound boneless lamb shoulder or leg

1 pound carrots, peeled and thickly sliced

1 pound new potatoes, cubed, skins left on

cold butter

Advance Preparation: The curing of the lamb will require 3 days before cooking.

1. Mix the salt, sugar, and dill. Rub this all over the lamb and place in a large resealable plastic bag, expelling any trapped air. Allow the lamb to cure for 3 days in the refrigerator. Turn the meat each day in the brine that develops.

2. Thoroughly rinse off the lamb and place in a large pot. Add enough cold water to cover. Heat to a boil and then lower the heat to a simmer. Cook, partially covered, for 1½ hours.

3. Drain the liquid from the pot and add fresh water to the lamb. Toss in the carrots and potatoes and cook 20 minutes, or until the vegetable are tender.

4. To serve, slice the lamb and serve it separately with the carrots and potatoes topped with cold butter.

Notes: Slices of cold lamb make an excellent sandwich, especially for *Smørrebrød*. Other root vegetables, such as turnips, can be added along with the carrots and potatoes.

Lamb and Asparagus

Lam i Asparges

Asparagus is a popular vegetable in Denmark. It thrives in maritime regions as it is quite tolerant to salt and salt spray, ideal for a country comprised of a peninsula and numerous islands.

---

1 pound fresh asparagus	⅓ cup all-purpose flour
3-pound lamb shoulder	¼ cup heavy cream
1 tablespoon salt	salt and pepper to taste
⅓ cup butter	

Advance Preparation: Remove the tough portion of each asparagus spear by bending the spear and allowing it to snap where it will. Reserve the tough stalks. Peel the trimmed asparagus with a vegetable peeler. Tie the asparagus trimmings and ends in a pouch of muslin.

1. Place the lamb in a pot and cover with cold water. Add the muslin pouch to the pot. Add the salt and heat to a boil. Immediately lower the heat to a simmer. Cook partially covered for 1½ hours, or until the meat is tender.

2. Add the asparagus spears and cook until tender, about 5 minutes.

3. Remove the meat and asparagus to a warm platter. Strain the cooking liquid and reserve 3 cups.

4. In a saucepan melt the butter over low heat. Whisk in the flour and cook the roux for 3 minutes, being careful not to brown the flour.

5. Whisk in the reserved 3 cups of cooking liquid and bring to a simmer. Cook 3 to 4 minutes. Whisk in the cream and cook 2 minutes. Adjust seasoning with salt and pepper.

6. Slice the lamb and top with asparagus. Pour sauce over and serve immediately.

Notes: Canned asparagus may be used in a pinch. Drain the liquid and add it as part of the liquid used for the sauce. Add the drained asparagus just a minute before removing the lamb, just to warm.

Roast Reindeer or Venison

Rensdyrssteg eller Rådyr

While many Americans would not blink if offered a venison roast, those same people may be repulsed by the thought of eating reindeer. Our Christmas traditions, including singing "Rudolph the Red-Nosed Reindeer," may have something to do with this. In the Stone Age, survival of the Danes was based on following the reindeer herds. Today, Greenland's *Kalaallit* (native Inuit tribe) still survive because of the reindeer.

---

1 small leg of reindeer or venison (about 8 pounds)
1 cup light oil, such as canola
1 tablespoon salt
2 teaspoons fresh ground pepper
1 teaspoon ground ginger
2 cups dry red wine
1 tablespoon whole allspice berries

2 bay leaves
1 lemon, thinly sliced
1 cup cream
2 tablespoons black currant or lingonberry jelly
2 eggs, separated
salt and pepper to taste

Advance Preparation: Heat the oven to 450 degrees F.

1. Rub the venison leg with oil. Place it in a roasting pan and brown the leg in a hot oven for 10 minutes, turning once. Lower the oven heat to 300 degrees F.

2. Mix the salt, ground pepper, and ginger. Sprinkle this over the browned venison leg.

3. Heat the red wine with the allspice, bay leaves, and lemon slices until aromatic, about 3 minutes. Pour this over the roast. Add 1 cup water. Cover the pan with foil and bake at 300 degrees F for 3 hours, turning the roast occasionally.

4. Remove the roasted leg to a warm platter and cover with foil. Strain the pan juices into a saucepan. Add the cream and boil the liquid until thick enough to coat the back of a spoon. Whisk in the jelly.

5. Whip the egg whites to form soft peaks. Beat the egg yolks with some of the hot cream sauce and then whisk into the cream sauce. Fold in the beaten whites. Adjust seasoning with salt and pepper.

6. Serve slices of roast with sauce on the side.

Notes: Other cuts of venison work well in this recipe. A bone-in loin would require about 30 to 45 minutes less roasting time.

Liver Pâté

Leverpostej

This delicious sandwich spread is a must for serving *Smørrebrød*. In winter, Danes place strips of jellied consommé and pickled cucumber slices on top. In summer, a cucumber salad is served on the side.

1½ pounds fresh pork liver

6 slices bacon, divided

1 medium onion, peeled and quartered

3 tablespoons butter

3 tablespoons all-purpose flour

1 cup warm cream

2 eggs

1 tablespoon salt

1 teaspoon freshly ground pepper

¼ teaspoon ground allspice

⅛ teaspoon ground cloves

Advance Preparation: Heat the oven to 325 degrees F.

1. Pass the liver and 4 strips of the bacon through a meat grinder. Add the onion and pass through a meat grinder twice more. The mixture should be a smooth paste.

2. Melt the butter over low heat. Whisk in the flour and cook 2 minutes, being careful not to brown the flour. Whisk in the warm cream and cook until thickened. Allow the sauce to simmer 2 minutes.

3. Beat the eggs with a portion of the hot sauce and then stir this into the cream sauce. Mix in the salt, pepper, allspice, and cloves. Allow to cool.

4. Mix the cream sauce with the ground liver mixture to form a smooth paste. Pour this into a buttered 8-inch loaf pan and set into a pan of water.

5. Top the loaf with the remaining 2 strips of bacon and bake for 1½ hours. Allow to cool and then refrigerate until thoroughly chilled. The spread is now ready to use.

Notes: Calves' liver may replace part or all of the pork liver. A food processor may be used in place of the meat grinder but be sure to have all ingredients chilled before processing.

Head Cheese

Sylte

As the name implies, this tasty loaf is made from the meat extracted from a pig's head. A more updated version (the one used here) avoids the awkward and inconvenient purchase and cooking of a pig's head, for more common and easily accessible pork cuts. However the taste will be inferior to the richly flavored meat of the head.

3 pounds pork shoulder, divided into 3 pieces
2 pork shanks
2 veal shanks
2 tablespoons salt
1 teaspoon freshly ground pepper
1 teaspoon ground allspice
¼ teaspoon ground nutmeg

Advance Preparation: The head cheese will need to be refrigerated overnight before use.

1. Place the pork shoulder, pork shanks, and veal shanks in a heavy pot. Add cold water to cover and cook 2 to 3 hours over low heat until the meat falls from the bones. Allow to cool and pull the meat from the bones.

2. Mix together the salt, pepper, allspice, and nutmeg.

3. Line a 8-inch loaf pan with cheesecloth, with enough to hang over the sides.

4. Add a layer of the pulled meat to the loaf pan and sprinkle with some of the spice mixture. Repeat until all of the meat is used.

5. Fold the cheesecloth over the top of the loaf pan and press down firmly to compact the filling. Set a heavy weight on top and refrigerate 24 hours. Slice thinly for sandwiches or *Smørrebrød*.

Notes: If a pig's head is available, simmer the whole head in a large pot of water for 3 hours. Skin the head and carefully pull the meat from the bones. Peel the tongue and slice. Use as directed above.

Creamed Sweetbreads

Brisselstuvning

Of the organ meats, sweetbreads are considered the most delicate and flavorful. They are the thymus glands of animals, and veal sweetbreads are considered to be the very best.

---

1 pound veal sweetbreads, cleaned with blood vessels removed

juice of 2 lemons, divided

salt

3 tablespoons butter plus additional for sautéing

3 tablespoons all-purpose flour

1 cup cream

ground pepper

toast points, rusks, or puff pastry shells

Advance Preparation: Place the sweetbreads in a pan of cold water. Add the juice of 1 lemon and a pinch of salt and heat to a boil. Lower the heat and simmer 15 minutes. Remove the sweetbreads and reserve 1½ cups of the poaching liquid. Allow the sweetbreads to cool 5 minutes. Can be done one day in advance.

1. Carefully peel the membrane around the surface of the cooked sweetbreads. Place the sweetbreads on a plate and add a heavy weight to compress them as they cool completely.

2. Dice the cooled sweetbreads and sauté them in some butter over medium heat until just crisp on the edges. Reserve, keeping warm.

3. Melt 3 tablespoons butter in the same pan and then stir in the flour. Cook over low heat 2 to 3 minutes, being careful not to brown the flour.

4. Whisk in the reserved poaching liquid and the juice of the remaining lemon, and cook over low heat until the sauce is simmering. Continue to cook for 5 minutes. Stir in the cream and cook 5 minutes, until thickened.

5. Add the sweetbreads and cook 2 minutes. Adjust seasoning with salt and pepper. Serve on toast points, rusks, or puff pastry shells.

Notes: A tasty and traditional addition to this recipe would be sautéed mushrooms. Sauté 4 ounces of sliced mushrooms in butter and add them, along with any pan juices, to the sauce when adding the sweetbreads.

Roast Marinated Rabbit

Serves 4

Marineret Stegt Hare

Of the Scandinavian countries, Denmark has the richest tradition of hunting and eating game. In addition to suitable land for game to thrive, the habits of Danish royalty have allowed for the filtering down of its culinary heritage to the common man.

1 bottle dry red wine

2 bay leaves

2 tablespoons allspice berries, crushed

2 tablespoons juniper berries, crushed

1 sprig fresh thyme

1 rabbit (about 4 pounds), dressed

1 medium onion, peeled and quartered

2 large carrots, peeled and thickly sliced

fresh watercress

Advance Preparation: Mix the red wine with the bay leaves, allspice berries, juniper berries, and thyme. Place the rabbit and the marinade in a resealable plastic bag. Refrigerate for 24 to 48 hours.

1. Heat oven to 450 degrees F. Remove the rabbit from the marinade and pat it dry, reserving the marinade. Put the marinated rabbit into a roasting pan and place in the oven for 10 minutes to brown.

2. Lower the oven heat to 350 degrees F and add the onion and carrots to the roasting pan. Pour the reserved marinade over the rabbit and roast about 1 hour, or until the rabbit is just done (the internal temperature of the thigh should be about 150 degrees F).

3. Allow the rabbit to cool for 5 minutes and then cut into pieces to serve. Strain the pan juices and thicken slightly with flour, if desired. Serve the rabbit and carrots on a platter garnished with watercress with the juices on the side.

Notes: The rabbit may be sectioned before marinating. Reduce cooking time by 20 minutes.

Poultry and Egg Dishes

The demand for quality eggs is high in a country with a baking tradition as famous as that of Denmark's. In addition to baked goods, eggs are used to enrich sauces and to make decadent savory and sweet custards and puddings. Until the beginning of the 1990s, there was little interest in fresh-killed chickens for the table. A survey of recipes written over the past 60 years shows few chicken dishes. This is changing with eating habits moving toward healthier, lower saturated fat dishes. As with all of Denmark's meats, Danish poultry is considered superior, with the lowest incidence of salmonella and other diseases related to poultry production.

More so than in other Scandinavian countries, Denmark's larder includes game and game birds. Waterfowl such as ducks and geese are among the most popular birds for the dinner table, and the Christmas goose is certainly featured on the holiday menu. Hunters from all around come for the many pheasant to be bagged in Denmark's lush countryside. Annual hunts are still a tradition among Danish royalty, and the dinner table is crowded with pheasant, duck, and goose, along with hare and venison, all from the same outing.

Chicken with Asparagus and Shrimp Sauce (Høns i Asperges og Rejer)

Chicken Salad (Hønsesalat)

Chicken with Rice (Høne i Ris)

Duck Cooked in Cream (Vildœnder)

Roast Goose with Apples and Prunes (Gåsesteg med Æbler og Svesker)

Roast Pheasant (Fasansteg)

Pickled Eggs (Eddikeæg)

Savory Egg Custard (Æggestand)

Eggs in Madeira Sauce (Spejlaeg I Madeirasky)

Pork Omelet (Flæskeæggekage)

Smoked Herring Omelet (Bornholmeræggekage)

Blue Cheese Omelet (Danabluæggekge)

Høns i Asperges og Rejer

The pairing of asparagus and shrimp to complement a meat dish is very Danish. Fresh asparagus should be sought for this recipe, although quality prepared asparagus in a glass jar could suffice in a pinch.

---

1 large chicken (4 to 5 pounds), quartered
1 medium onion, diced
¼ cup canola oil
2 bay leaves
1 tablespoon whole peppercorns
1 pound fresh asparagus, coarse ends of stalks removed, peeled

3 tablespoons butter
3 tablespoons all-purpose flour
8 ounces cooked and peeled small shrimp
2 egg yolks
salt and pepper to taste

Advance Preparation: All advance preparation may be found in the ingredient list.

1. In a large pot, brown the chicken and onion in the oil over medium heat. Cover the chicken with cold water and add the bay leaves and peppercorns. Heat to a boil and then lower the heat to a simmer. Cook 1 hour, partially covered, skimming the surface as needed. Remove the chicken to a warm plate and strain the cooking liquid. Reserve 1 cup.

2. Put the asparagus in a skillet and cover with 2 cups water. Heat to a boil and then lower the heat to a simmer. Cook about 5 minutes or until just tender. Reserve 1 cup cooking liquid.

3. Melt the butter in a saucepan over low heat. Add the flour and cook 3 minutes, being careful not to brown the flour. Add the reserved cooking liquids, a total of 2 cups, and whisk to combine. Heat to a boil and then lower the heat and simmer 3 minutes, stirring occasionally. Add the cooked shrimp.

4. Beat the egg yolks with some of the hot sauce. Stir this back into the sauce and heat very gently for 1 minute, being careful not to curdle the eggs.

5. Add the chicken and asparagus and continue to heat gently for 1 minute. Adjust seasoning with salt and pepper. Serve immediately.

Notes: If using jarred asparagus, reserve the liquid to use in the sauce. The egg yolks may be replaced with ½ cup cream. Add this with the cooking liquids and extend cooking time to 5 minutes.

Chicken Salad

Serves 4 to 6

Hønsesalat

There's chicken salad and then there is the Danish way to make chicken salad—using whipped heavy cream instead of the usual mayonnaise.

2 cups cubed cooked chicken breast	1 teaspoon prepared mustard
1 cup finely diced celery	1 cup heavy cream
½ cup chopped fresh dill, some stems included	salt and pepper to taste

Advance Preparation: The chicken will have to be cooked ahead of time, if not using leftovers, and then chilled.

1. Toss the chicken with the celery and dill. Stir in the mustard.
2. Whip the cream to stiff peaks.
3. Fold the whipped cream into the chicken mixture. Adjust seasoning with salt and pepper.

Notes: This salad can be used for *Smørrebrød* or placed into lettuce "cups" to serve as a salad. Garnish with capers and tomato slices.

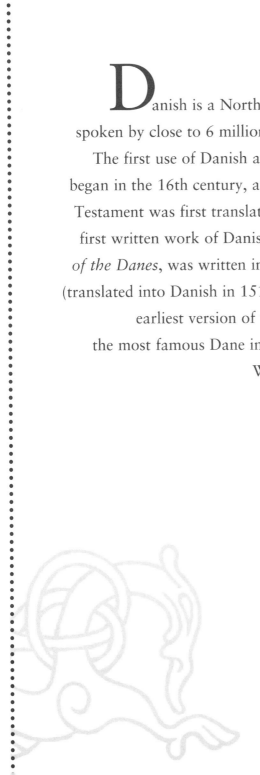

Danish is a North Germanic language spoken by close to 6 million people worldwide. The first use of Danish as a literary language began in the 16th century, and in 1531 the New Testament was first translated into Danish. The first written work of Danish literature, *History of the Danes*, was written in Latin around 1200 (translated into Danish in 1514) and included the earliest version of the story of Hamlet, the most famous Dane in literature thanks to William Shakespeare.

Chicken with Rice

Serves 4 to 6

Høne i Ris

Unlike most chicken-and-rice dishes, this recipe uses a prepared rice mixture as an encasement for the chicken, forming a crusty dome when baked. A steam vent is formed in the rice before baking and the crusting is encouraged by brushing with beaten egg.

1 large roasting chicken, about 4 pounds, cut into serving-size pieces (see Notes)	salt and pepper to taste
6 tablespoons butter, softened, plus 2 tablespoons butter, melted	3 cups cooked rice
	2 teaspoons sugar
4 tablespoons all-purpose flour	½ cup chopped skinless almonds
pinch nutmeg	3 eggs, beaten
	½ cup unseasoned dry breadcrumbs

Advance Preparation: The rice will need to be cooked ahead of time, if not leftover, and then cooled. Heat oven to 350 degrees F.

1. Place the chicken pieces in a large pot. Cover with water and heat to a boil. Lower the heat and simmer, uncovered, for 40 minutes, skimming as needed. Remove the chicken to a warm platter, strain the cooking liquid and reserve 2 cups.

2. Melt 4 tablespoons of the softened butter in a saucepan and stir in the flour. Cook over low heat 3 minutes, being careful not to brown the flour. Whisk in the 2 cups reserved cooking liquid and heat to a boil. Lower the heat and simmer 2 minutes. Add the nutmeg and adjust seasoning with salt and pepper.

3. Mix the cooked rice with the remaining 2 tablespoons softened butter, sugar, and almonds. Reserve 2 tablespoons of the beaten egg and stir the rest into the rice mixture.

4. Put the cooked chicken in a large roasting pan. Spoon the rice mixture over the chicken, covering all of the pieces. Pat firm with moistened hands, forming a crust. Form a vent hole in the center.

5. Bake at 350 degrees F for 1 hour. Remove the pan from the oven and raise the heat to 425 degrees F. Brush the surface of the rice with the reserved egg.

6. Mix the breadcrumbs with the melted butter and top the rice with this mixture. Return the pan to the oven and bake until a brown, crisp crust forms, about 5 minutes. Allow to cool 5 minutes before serving.

Notes: To cut up a chicken into 8 serving pieces, divide each breast into 2 pieces. Remove the wing tips and leave the "drumettes" on the breast pieces. Separate the thighs from the legs.

Duck Cooked in Cream

Serves 4

Vildœnder

Danish cuisine is known for using rich dairy products in copious amounts. The Danish countryside, often near water, is lush with waterfowl. But only the Danes would combine the two into one fabulous, fat-laden dish. A whole duck is covered in boiling cream and simmered until tender, and what remains in the pan after cooking becomes the sauce.

3 tablespoons butter

1 duckling (about 5 pounds), rinsed, patted dry, and left whole

6 cups cream

pinch nutmeg

salt and pepper to taste

1. Melt the butter in a deep pan just larger than the duck. Brown the duck in the butter, turning to brown all sides.

2. Heat the cream to boiling. Stir in the nutmeg and pour the boiling cream over the duck.

3. Cook, partially covered, over low heat 1 hour. Remove the duck to a carving board and slowly simmer the remaining liquid in the pan, uncovered, for 10 minutes, or until thickened. Adjust seasoning with salt and pepper.

4. To serve, section the duck into 4 pieces (2 breast and 2 leg/thigh) and serve the sauce separately.

Notes: Duck breasts may also be prepared in this manner. Use just enough cream to cover and reduce cooking time for the duck to 30 minutes.

Roast Goose with Apples and Prunes

Serves 8

Gåsesteg med Æbler og Svesker

Roast goose is customarily served on Christmas Eve, right after the rice pudding. Geese are eaten throughout the winter and young geese are available in markets as early as the end of June.

---

8 ounces dried plums (prunes)

4 medium tart apples, such as Granny Smith, peeled, cored, and sliced

1 goose (8 to 10 pounds), cleaned, excess fat removed

1 lemon, halved

salt

pepper

4 cups chicken or vegetable stock, heated to a simmer

flour

salt and pepper to taste

Advance Preparation: Plump the dried plums in hot water for 10 minutes. Heat the oven to 400 degrees F.

1. Toss the plumped dried plums with the apple slices.

2. Rub the skin of the goose with the cut lemon. Sprinkle with salt and pepper. Loosely stuff the bird with the apple mixture and close the opening with skewers or twine. Truss the bird, if desired. Prick the skin all over, being careful not to pierce the flesh (pull the skin up and away from the flesh with your fingers before piercing).

3. Place the bird on its side in a roasting pan and roast for 30 minutes. Pour off the accumulated fat from the pan and pour the heated stock over the goose. Roast an additional 1½ hours, basting occasionally.

4. Turn the bird to the other side and roast an additional 1 hour. Drain off the pan juices and reserve and let cool to allow the fat to separate. Roast goose an additional 20 minutes. Pour some cold water over the skin of the goose and roast an additional 10 minutes to crisp the skin. Allow the goose to cool for 20 minutes before carving. During that time make the gravy.

5. Skim the fat from the reserved pan juices and heat the liquid to a simmer. Mix some flour with cold water to form a paste. Stir portions of the flour paste into the simmering liquid to thicken to desired consistency. Simmer 2 additional minutes to remove any raw flour taste. Adjust seasoning with salt and pepper.

6. Remove the fruit stuffing to serve alongside and then carve the goose. Serve with the gravy.

Notes: A duckling may be prepared as above, serving 4 persons (make a half recipe of stuffing). Coarsely chopped walnuts make a tasty addition to the stuffing. Other dried fruit, such as apricots, can replace some or all of the dried plums.

Roast Pheasant

Fasansteg

It is known across Europe that Denmark is the premier place to hunt pheasants. There are organized hunts that include the traditional horn-blowing to start the hunt, finishing with a dinner of the larder bagged during the hunt. The island of Langeland is one of the best places in Denmark to hunt game birds.

2 small pheasants, dressed and halved down the back

4 tablespoons butter

salt and pepper

2 cups dry white wine

Advance Preparation: Heat the oven to 350 degrees F.

1. In a large roasting pan, brown the pheasant halves in butter. Turn them skin-side up and dust with salt and pepper.

2. Add the wine and bring the liquid to a boil. Remove the pan from the heat and cover with foil. Place it into the heated oven and braise for 1½ hours.

3. Remove the foil and roast an additional 1 hour. Remove the pheasants to a warm platter and strain the pan juices.

4. Serve a half pheasant per person, with pan juices drizzled over.

Notes: The pheasant halves may be stuffed before braising. Melt 1 pound of butter with ¼ cup cream and stir in 4 cups fresh breadcrumbs. Add salt and pepper and stir in 3 egg yolks. Stuff the cavity of each half with portions of this stuffing *(Fyld til Småfugle).*

Pickled Eggs

Eddikeæg

No food can escape the Danish love for pickling, and eggs make an excellent medium for this method. They are served on the *Smørgåsbord* table and to accompany sandwiches and snacks.

2 dozen hard-boiled eggs, shells removed

3 cups cider vinegar

1 tablespoon whole allspice berries

1 teaspoon ground ginger

2 small bay leaves

Advance Preparation: These eggs should be made 48 hours in advance of serving.

1. Place the eggs in a large glass jar.

2. Heat the vinegar to a boil with the allspice, ginger, and bay leaves. Lower the heat and simmer until aromatic, about 5 minutes.

3. Pour the hot vinegar, along with the spices, over the eggs and allow to cool uncovered. When cool, seal tightly and allow to stand at room temperature 48 hours.

Notes: Whole cloves may replace some of the allspice. Add some blanched carrots to the jar for color and crunch.

Savory Egg Custard

Æggestand

Rich custards made from the freshest eggs, laid by contented chickens, are popular fare for a *Smørrebrød* lunch as the baked custard will not soak sandwich bread the way scrambled eggs would. The custard can also be cut into fanciful shapes and added as garnish to soups.

4 large eggs, at room temperature   ½ teaspoon salt
1 cup half and half or light cream   fresh grated nutmeg
fresh ground pepper

Advance Preparation: Heat the oven to 325 degrees F. Bring some water to a boil for the water bath.

1. Gently whisk the eggs and stir in the half and half. Add a few twists of black pepper, the salt, and a couple of gratings of nutmeg (be careful not to overdo the nutmeg).

2. Place the custard into a 2-cup buttered baking dish. Place the baking dish in another pan slightly larger than the baking dish.

3. Place the pans in the oven and carefully pour boiling water into the larger pan, having the water come three-quarters up the sides of the baking dish.

4. Bake the custard for 20 minutes, or until just set in the center. The point of a knife should come out clean from the center of the custard. Remove from the oven and the water bath, and allow the custard to cool on a wire rack.

5. Unmold and cut into desired shapes or serving pieces.

Notes: To make a tasty luncheon dish or appetizer, add cooked meats, fish, or shellfish, or blanched vegetables to the custard before baking. Unmold and serve portions with buttered dark rye bread.

Eggs in Madeira Sauce

Serves 4

Spejlaeg I Madeirasky

Many Danish egg dishes are eaten as luncheon items rather than for breakfast. This dish of fried eggs in rich Madeira sauce is an example of traditional Danish restaurant fare.

1 cup rich meat stock	4 slices Canadian bacon or ham
2 tablespoons Madeira or dry Sherry	4 pieces toasted light bread
dash Worcestershire sauce	4 fried eggs

Advance Preparation: All advance preparation may be found in the ingredient list.

1. Heat the stock to a simmer. Add the Madeira and Worcestershire sauce and cook 2 minutes over low heat.

2. Place a slice of Canadian bacon on each piece of toasted bread. Top each with a fried egg.

3. To serve pour Madeira sauce over and serve immediately.

Notes: Sauce may be thickened with a slurry of potato starch or cornstarch in water, if desired.

There is a festival held in the Faroe Islands which creates much controversy year after year. It is a cultural event appreciated by few beyond the coastlines of the islands. *Grindadráp* is the pilot whale and dolphin festival, where a number of these aquatic mammals are killed ceremoniously to provide meat and blubber to the communities throughout the islands. The Faroese say that about 25 percent of their annual meat consumption comes from the festival and that the animals are humanely killed with little suffering. Conservationists, animal-rights groups, and the Whaling Commission disagree, labeling it a slaughter unnecessary in these modern times and a practice that should be banned. Ironically pollution has made the consumption of the whale meat dangerous due to high levels of toxins, so much so that medical officers of the Faroe Islands recommend an end to the practice.

Pork Omelet

Flæskeæggekage

Streaky pork is called for in the original recipes for this dish, and there is really no American cut of pork that is equivalent. Unsmoked bacon would be closest to the Danish product.

8 ounces streaky pork or unsmoked bacon, sliced

4 eggs

1 tablespoon potato starch or cornstarch

½ cup light cream or half and half

freshly ground pepper

2 small ripe tomatoes, quartered

chopped chives

Advance Preparation: There is no advance preparation for this dish.

1. Fry the pork or bacon in a heavy skillet until crisp. Remove meat from the pan. Pour off half of the pan drippings.

2. Whisk the eggs with the potato starch and cream. Add a few twists of pepper.

3. Heat the skillet and drippings and pour in the beaten egg mixture. Allow it to cook for 1 minute, pushing in the sides to allow uncooked egg to run under the omelet.

4. Arrange the tomato quarters and cooked pork strips on the surface of the omelet.

5. Place the pan under a broiler to finish off the top of the omelet. Sprinkle with chopped chives and serve immediately.

Notes: Prepared mustard often accompanies this omelet in Denmark, along with buttered dark rye bread.

Smoked Herring Omelet

Serves 4

Bornholmeræggekage

The Danish name of this omelet reflects the island of Bornholm, famous for its superior herrings and smoked herring products. Bornholm is Denmark's only rocky island.

8 eggs
1 cup light cream or half and half
pinch salt
butter for frying

8 smoked herring fillets
4 radishes, thinly sliced
chopped chives

Advance Preparation: If using whole smoked herrings, fillet them before starting the omelet.

1. Whisk the eggs with the cream and salt.

2. Heat some butter in a large heavy skillet over medium heat. Pour in the egg mixture and cook over low heat, scrambling the eggs briefly to lighten them.

3. As the eggs set, arrange the herring fillets on top in a wheel spoke pattern. Place radish slices between.

4. Continue to cook over very low heat until the omelet is set. Serve hot right from the skillet, garnished with chopped chives.

Notes: In some regions shredded lettuce tops the omelet. Chopped scallions can replace the chives.

Blue Cheese Omelet

Serves 4

Danabluæggekge

Danish blue cheese, called *Danablu*, was developed around the turn of the 20th century, using the inoculant *Penicillium roquefort*, the same as used in the finest of blue cheeses. *Danablu* is crumbly and soft, with a sharp and salty undertone.

---

8 large eggs

1 cup whole milk

½ teaspoon salt

freshly ground black pepper

butter for frying

4 ounces Danish blue cheese, crumbled

chopped fresh dill

Advance Preparation: Have a broiler ready, using medium heat.

1. Whisk the eggs until frothy. Stir in the milk. Add the salt and a few twists of black pepper.

2. Heat a large heavy skillet and add some butter. When it foams, pour in the eggs.

3. Cook over medium-high heat, pressing the edges to the center, allowing liquid to run under the omelet to cook.

4. Distribute the crumbled blue cheese across the surface. Place the omelet under the broiler to brown. Serve immediately, topped with chopped dill.

Notes: The omelet may be turned with a spatula, but the broiler will avoid predictable disasters. The dill may be stirred into the eggs before cooking.

Vegetables and Side Dishes

Over 60 percent of the land in Denmark is arable, and with a temperate climate and sufficient rain evenly distributed, crops thrive in Denmark's short growing season. In addition to feed for the pigs and dairy cows, cold-weather-friendly crops that store well over drawn-out winters are produced on small farms and in backyard gardens. Root vegetables and cruciferous crops, such as cabbages and kale, form the principal side dishes. Potatoes, beets, cabbages, mustard greens, and kale are the foundation of Danish vegetable recipes. With much decaying wood on forest floors, mushrooms are enthusiastically hunted and, of course, enjoyed in many dishes.

Caramelized Potatoes (Brunede Kartofler)

Bacon and Potatoes (Braendende Kaerlighed)

Scalloped Potatoes and Anchovies (Kartofler med Ansjos)

Pickled Beets (Sylte Rødbeder)

Gingered Beets (Rødbeder i Ingefærsauce)

Glazed Shallots (Glaserede Løg)

Red Cabbage (Rødkål)

Browned Cabbage (Brunkål)

Cabbage with Caraway (Hvidkål med Kommen)

Creamed Kale (Gronkaal med Fløde)

Fried Tomatoes (Stegte Tomater)

Cauliflower with Cheese Sauce (Blomkaal med Ostesauce)

Creamed Mushrooms (Champignonstuvning)

Caramelized Potatoes

Serves 4

Brunede Kartofler

This is the favorite way potatoes are prepared in Denmark. Their sugar glaze makes them irresistible to serve with pork, poultry, and other meats.

2 pounds "C-size" new potatoes (uniformly small, about the size of an egg or slightly smaller)	3 tablespoons sugar
	½ teaspoon salt
3 tablespoons butter	chopped parsley

Advance Preparation: Boil the new potatoes in sufficient salted water until tender, about 10 minutes. Allow to cool.

1. Peel the cooked potatoes.

2. Heat the butter in a heavy skillet until it foams. Add the sugar and stir constantly until the sugar begins to brown.

3. Toss in the potatoes and stir to coat them. Cook over low heat until the potatoes are hot and glazed.

4. Add the salt and parsley and toss together. Serve immediately.

Notes: Other small potatoes, such as fingerlings, would be delicious prepared in this manner. If "C-size" potatoes are not available, pick through new potatoes for the smallest ones, being careful to select those of uniform size.

Burning Passion

Brændende Kærlighed

No one is sure of why this dish is named as it is, but it is an old Danish country recipe that is quite popular. It's an excellent way to use leftover mashed potatoes.

4 medium onions, sliced thin	salt
4 tablespoons butter	2 cups leftover mashed potatoes
12 ounces fatty pork, cut into small cubes	1 cup pickled beets, diced

Advance Preparation: If no leftover mashed potatoes are on hand, cook 2 pounds of peeled potatoes and mash them with some butter and cream. Season with salt and pepper. Reserve until needed.

1. Fry the onions in the butter until golden and crisp. Remove them, leaving the butter in the pan.

2. Fry the pork cubes in the butter used for the onions until crisp and browned, adding more butter if necessary. Sprinkle with salt.

3. Heat the mashed potatoes in a microwave and place them in a warm 10-inch casserole dish, making a well in the center. Add the cooked pork to the well and top with the fried onions.

4. Scatter the diced beets around the border and serve immediately.

Notes: Pork belly works nicely for this dish. Streaky bacon can be used, but omit the salt.

Scalloped Potatoes with Anchovies

Serves 4

Kartofler med Ansjos

Everyone likes scalloped potatoes and this version offers a Scandinavian twist. Anchovy fillets are chopped and added to the potatoes before baking, infusing the dish with a briny quality.

2 pounds potatoes, peeled and thinly sliced	2 tablespoons butter
salt and pepper	6 anchovy fillets, packed in salt, rinsed, and coarsely chopped
¼ cup diced onions	1 cup light cream or half and half, warmed
¼ cup unseasoned dry breadcrumbs	

Advance Preparation: Heat the oven to 350 degrees F.

1. Layer half of the sliced potatoes in a baking dish. Sprinkle with salt and pepper.

2. Sprinkle the onions over and then the breadcrumbs. Dot with butter.

3. Add the chopped anchovies and top with the remaining potatoes. Carefully pour in the warm cream.

4. Cover the dish and bake at 350 degrees F for 30 minutes. Lower the oven to 325 degrees F and remove the cover. Bake an additional 30 minutes or until golden brown. Serve immediately.

Notes: Anchovies packed in salt are preferable and will look like tiny filleted fish. They can often be found in upscale markets. If using anchovies packed in oil, drain thoroughly.

Pickled Beets

Serves 4 to 6

Sylte Rødbeder

Pickled beets are found on the Smørgåsbord table and served with *Smørrebrød* sandwiches and as a participant on a relish and pickle tray to accompany meats.

2 pounds beets, greens removed and trimmed	1 teaspoon salt
2 cups red wine vinegar	1 teaspoon whole cloves
3 cups sugar	

Advance Preparation: This recipe will benefit from resting in the refrigerator overnight.

1. Simmer the beets in enough water to cover for 40 minutes, or until the beets are fork tender. Allow them to cool.

2. Peel the beets by sliding off the skins, which should come off easily. Slice the beets and place them in a glass jar or other non-reactive container.

3. Heat the vinegar to boiling and then lower the heat to a simmer. Stir in the sugar to dissolve. Add the salt.

4. Pour the hot liquid over the beets and add the whole cloves. Allow to cool. Refrigerate, covered, overnight.

Notes: A piece of fresh horseradish root may be added along with the cloves. Cider vinegar may replace red wine vinegar.

Gingered Beets

Rødbeder i Ingefærsauce

Beets are one of two major crops in Denmark, the other being potatoes. In addition to accompanying sandwiches and complementing meat dishes, beets are grown for sugar production.

2 pounds beets, greens removed	2 teaspoons cornstarch
2 teaspoons grated fresh ginger	4 tablespoons butter
⅔ cup sugar	salt and pepper to taste
⅓ cup vinegar	

Advance Preparation: Simmer the beets in salted water until tender, about 30 minutes. Reserve ½ cup of the cooking liquid. Allow the beets to cool and peel by slipping off the skins.

1. Cut the cooled beets into bite-size pieces.

2. In a non-reactive pan mix the reserved cooking liquid, ginger, sugar, vinegar, and cornstarch. Whisk to combine. Cook over low heat until the sugar dissolves and the sauce thickens, about 5 minutes.

3. Stir in the butter and the prepared beets. Cook 2 minutes over low heat. Remove from the heat and season to taste with salt and pepper. Serve immediately.

Notes: If fresh ginger is not available, 1 teaspoon of ground ginger may substitute. You may top the dish with chopped dill or parsley before serving.

Glazed Shallots

Glaserede Løg

Glazed vegetables with their caramelized coating are quite popular in Denmark. Danes love their pork, and the sweetness of a caramel glaze is the perfect complement to ham, roast pork, and smoked pork loin.

2 tablespoons butter
2 tablespoons sugar
1 pound shallots, peeled (select
    those of uniform size)

salt to taste

Advance Preparation: To easily peel the shallots, trim the root ends and blanch them briefly in boiling water.

1. Heat the butter over medium heat until it foams. Stir in the sugar and cook over low heat until the sugar turns a golden brown but does not burn.

2. Add the peeled shallots and cook over low heat until the shallots are uniformly glazed, about 3 minutes.

3. Add enough water to just cover the shallots and simmer over low heat until the shallots are tender but retain their shape, about 20 minutes. The water should have mostly evaporated and the shallots should be coated with a glossy, sugary glaze. Add salt to taste and serve immediately.

Notes: Other small onions, such as pearl onions or cippoline would be excellent in this dish. Carrots are also delicious prepared in this manner. Peel 1 pound of carrots and cut them into thick rounds. Use a cooking time in water of 8 to 10 minutes.

Red Cabbage

Rødkål

In addition to being one of the most popular winter vegetables enjoyed across Scandinavia, red cabbage is usually served for Christmas dinner in Denmark. It goes particularly well with roast goose and duck.

1 medium head red cabbage (about 3 pounds)
2 tart apples, such as Granny Smith
butter
½ cup cider vinegar

⅓ cup red currant jelly
sugar to taste
salt and pepper

Advance Preparation: This recipe should be made one day in advance for enhanced flavor.

1. Remove the outer leaves from the cabbage and cut the head into quarters. Remove the cores and finely shred the cabbage.

2. Peel, core, and grate the apples.

3. Heat some butter in a large non-reactive skillet. Sauté the cabbage and apples over low heat for 5 minutes.

4. Add the vinegar and ½ cup water and simmer until the cabbage is tender, about 10 minutes.

5. Stir in the red currant jelly and adjust sweetness with additional sugar. Add salt and pepper to taste. Serve warm.

Notes: To enhance the color of the cooked cabbage, ¼ cup of beet juice (reserved from canned beets) may be added with the jelly.

Pickled Herring Salad, page 29

Cured Salmon (Gravlaks), page 50

Fried Pork Belly with Apples, page 71

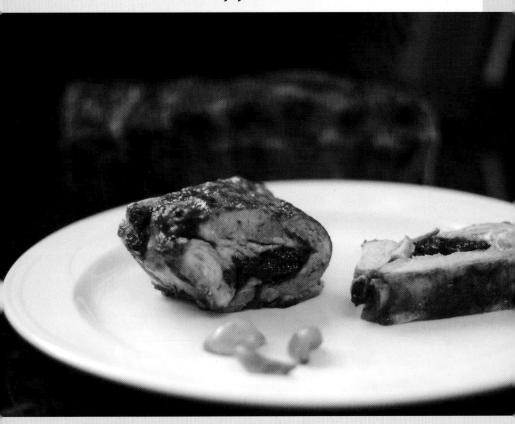

Roast Spare Ribs
with Apples and Prunes, page 74

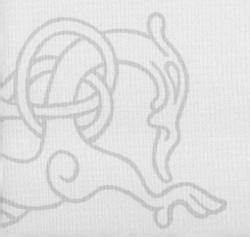

Minced Beefsteak with Onions, page 81

Cabbage Rolls, page 87

Chicken with Asparagus and Shrimp Sauce, page 97

Blue Cheese Omelet, page 110

Old-Fashioned Danish Black Bread, page 149

Danish Pastry Dough
and Danish Pastries, page 161

Kringle, page 164

Danish Doughnuts, page 169

Sour Cream Chocolate Cake, page 184

Sour Cream Cookies, page 195

Browned Cabbage

Brunkål

It is said that even those that do not like cabbage love this dish.

---

1 medium head green cabbage
 (about 3 pounds)
3 tablespoons butter

3 tablespoons sugar
salt to taste

Advance Preparation: Remove the outer leaves from the cabbage and cut the head into quarters. Remove the cores and finely shred the cabbage, as for cole slaw.

1. Melt the butter in a large, heavy skillet. Add the sugar and cook over medium heat until the mixture browns. Add the cabbage and sauté until the cabbage is browned, about 3 minutes.

2. Add enough water to just cover the cabbage, cover and simmer over very low heat for 1 hour, adding water as necessary.

3. Remove the lid and continue to cook until there is almost no liquid left in the pan. Adjust seasoning with salt and then serve immediately.

Notes: A piece of salt pork may be added to the cabbage when adding the water to cover. Be careful when adjusting seasoning with salt, as the salt pork will bring a considerable amount to this dish.

Cabbage with Caraway

Hvidkål med Kommen

Caraway is one of the few spices readily used in Danish cuisine. It is present in Denmark's dark rye breads, and pairing it with cabbage has been traditional among northern European countries for centuries.

---

1 small head green cabbage (about 2 pounds or less)

2 tablespoons butter, melted

2 eggs

1 cup light cream or half and half

1 teaspoon caraway seeds

salt and pepper to taste

Advance Preparation: Remove the outer leaves from the cabbage and cut the head into quarters. Remove the cores and shred the cabbage. Soak the cabbage in ice water for 2 hours. Heat the oven to 350 degrees F.

1. Bring a large pot of water to a boil. Drain the cabbage and add to the boiling water and simmer 5 minutes. Drain thoroughly.

2. Mix the melted butter with the eggs and cream. Add the caraway seeds and stir in the cabbage.

3. Put in a buttered baking dish and bake for 30 minutes, or until bubbling and lightly browned on top.

4. Adjust seasoning with salt and pepper and serve immediately.

Notes: Crumbled cooked bacon may be added before baking.

Creamed Kale

Serves 4

Gronkaal med Fløde

Kale is in the cabbage family but its leaves do not form a head. It has been grown in Europe for centuries, being quite hardy, pest resistant, and tolerant of even the poorest soils. Its nutritional value is quite high, being rich in beta carotene, vitamin C, and calcium.

1 head kale, leaves separated, rinsed, and tough stems removed

3 tablespoons butter

3 tablespoons all-purpose flour

2 cups milk, warmed

2 hardboiled eggs, peeled and chopped

salt and pepper to taste

Advance Preparation: Blanch the kale leaves in salted water for 3 minutes. Drain, pat dry and chop.

1. Melt the butter over low heat in a saucepan. Whisk in the flour and cook 2 minutes, being careful not to brown the flour.

2. Whisk in the warm milk and cook over medium heat until simmering and thickened. Cook an additional 2 minutes.

3. Stir the chopped kale and eggs gently into the white sauce. Cook 1 minute over low heat.

4. Adjust seasoning with salt and pepper and serve immediately.

Notes: A few grindings of nutmeg would be a tasty addition to this dish.

Fried Tomatoes

Stegte Tomater

Whether juicy, ripe, and red, or firm, tart, and green, fried tomatoes are a favorite on the *Smørgåsbord* table and can be used to top a *Smørrebrød* sandwich. They make a tasty side dish for pork and poultry, and appreciate a glaze of flavorful sauce.

---

4 green tomatoes, cut into thick ¾-inch slices

flour for dredging

2 eggs, beaten with 1 tablespoon water

1 cup dry unseasoned breadcrumbs

8 tablespoons butter

salt and pepper

Advance Preparation: All advance preparation may be found in the ingredient list.

1. Dredge the tomato slices in flour, shaking off the excess.

2. Dip the tomato slices in egg wash and then into breadcrumbs. Allow to rest 2 minutes.

3. Melt the butter in a large heavy skillet. When it foams add the tomato slices, making sure not to crowd the pan (fry in batches if necessary).

4. Turn the slices once, browning on both sides. Remove the tomatoes to paper towels. Dust with salt and pepper and serve immediately.

Notes: For a traditional topping, serve the fried tomatoes topped with horseradish sauce (*Peberrodssauce*, page 130).

Cauliflower with Cheese Sauce

Blomkaal med Ostesauce

Garden-fresh vegetables are a highlight of Danish cooking. To preserve the beauty of cauliflower, it is often wrapped in cheesecloth before cooking. In this recipe, the cheese sauce is made with *Samsöe*, a Danish cheese similar to Ementhaler with the flavor of mild cheddar.

---

1 large head cauliflower, trimmed, left whole

cheesecloth

2 tablespoons butter

2 tablespoons all-purpose flour

1½ cups milk, warmed

2 egg yolks

½ cup grated Samsöe cheese

salt and pepper to taste

dry breadcrumbs

Advance Preparation: Wrap the cauliflower in cheesecloth and place it in a large pot. Cover with water and simmer until just tender, about 30 minutes. Heat the oven to 400 degrees F.

1. Melt the butter in a saucepan. Whisk in the flour and cook over low heat for 3 minutes, being careful not to brown the flour.

2. Whisk in the warm milk and heat to a boil. Lower the heat and simmer 2 minutes. Stir some of the hot sauce into the egg yolks to temper. Beat them into the sauce and cook over very low heat 2 minutes, being careful not to boil the sauce.

3. Stir in the cheese to blend and adjust seasoning with salt and pepper.

4. Remove the cauliflower from the cheesecloth and place in a baking dish. Top with sauce and dust with breadcrumbs. Bake until golden brown. Serve immediately from the baking dish.

Notes: Havarti cheese can replace the Samsöe if you want a Danish cheese for the recipe. Other non-Danish cheeses such as Ementhaler or mild cheddar can also be used.

Creamed Mushrooms

Champignonstuvning

Mushroom hunting season in Denmark runs from July through October. Pine forests are best, as the soft wood easily decays, providing a home for edible fungi. Chanterelles appear in late July with sufficient rain and the king bolete, also known as porcini, soon follows.

1 pound assorted mushrooms	juice of 1 lemon
4 tablespoons butter	salt to taste
1½ cups heavy cream	

Advance Preparation: Clean and trim the mushrooms (see Notes).

1. Slice the cleaned mushrooms.

2. Heat the butter in a sauté pan over medium heat until it foams. Add the mushrooms and sauté until they release their liquid, about 2 minutes.

3. Add the cream and cook until thickened and the sauce coats the back of a spoon.

4. Add the lemon juice and adjust seasoning with salt. Serve immediately.

Notes: To clean mushrooms use a towel or a brush to remove any dirt or growing medium. Never soak them in water, as it will be absorbed and make the surface of the mushrooms slimy. Trim the stems with a sharp knife.

T hose who have never visited Denmark mistakenly picture it as a winter wonderland, much like its Scandinavian neighbors. But Denmark's overall terrain is flat; its highest elevation is a mere 568 feet above sea level. At 482 feet, the second highest elevation, resides the optimistically named *Himmelbjergetor* or Heaven Mountain. As well, it rarely snows in this temperate climate. Denmark does not send a team to the Winter Olympics, and its major winter sports are indoor badminton and handball.

Sauces

Sauces are an expected accompaniment to meat dishes in Denmark. Few spices are used during cooking and the popular cooking method of boiling/simmering/poaching in water does not bring significant flavor to the table. Sauces come to the rescue, adding needed dimensions and depth. The cooking liquid is often used as the base for a sauce for the dish, concentrating the essence of the meat into the sauce. Sauces are typically roux-based or butter sauces. The most interesting "sauce" is striking in its simplicity—beaten butter. Exquisitely fresh quality butter is beaten for 15 minutes, turning almost white in color, with a remarkable texture and flavor that belies its simplicity. In addition to savory sauces, fruit sauces complement dessert custards and puddings.

Sour Cream Sauce (Sur Fløde Sauce)

Onion Sauce (Løgsovs)

Mustard Sauce (Sennepsauce)

Horseradish Sauce (Peberrodssauce)

Parsley Sauce (Persillesauce)

Dill Sauce (Dildsauce)

Mushroom Sauce (Champignonssauce)

Creamed Butter (Rørt Smør)

    Horseradish Butter (Peberrodssmør)

    Anchovy Butter (Ansjossmør)

    Dill Butter (Dildsmør)

    Lemon Butter (Citronsmør)

Drawn Butter Sauce (Smørsauce)

Fruit Sauce (Frugtsauce)

Cinnamon Sauce (Kanelsauce)

Cardamom Sauce (Kardemommesauce)

Sour Cream Sauce

Sur Fløde Sauce

This versatile sauce is delicious over cabbage and makes an excellent pairing with roast pork.

3 tablespoons bacon drippings or butter	1 cup sour cream, at room temperature
3 tablespoons all-purpose flour	salt and pepper to taste
1½ cups beef stock	

Advance Preparation: Bacon may have to be cooked if using drippings. Prepare a rich beef stock if not using a prepared stock.

1. Heat the bacon drippings in a saucepan and stir in the flour. Cook over low heat for 2 minutes, being careful not to brown the flour.

2. Add the beef stock and whisk to combine. Bring to a boil over medium heat. Lower the heat and simmer 3 minutes.

3. Just before serving, whisk in the sour cream and adjust seasoning with salt and pepper.

Notes: Quality canned beef broth may replace the homemade version. Bouillon cubes should be avoided at all cost.

Onion Sauce

Løgsovs

This sauce is usually referred to as "Onion Sauce for Herrings," but is delicious over boiled potatoes and steamed kale as well.

3 tablespoons butter

1 medium onion, finely diced

2 tablespoons all-purpose flour

1 cup light cream or half and half, heated

salt and pepper to taste (be conservative with salt if using the sauce over herrings)

Advance Preparation: Finely dice the onion; but if more texture is desired, just thinly slice it.

1. Melt the butter over low heat in a saucepan. Add the diced onion and sauté over medium heat until the onions are golden brown and aromatic.

2. Stir in the flour and cook over low heat 2 minutes.

3. Whisk in the warm cream and bring to a boil over low heat. Lower the heat and simmer 2 minutes.

4. Adjust seasoning with salt and pepper. Serve at once.

Notes: One cup of sliced shallots can replace the onion.

Mustard Sauce

Sennepsauce

This sauce is primarily served with boiled cod or fish patties and balls.

---

4 tablespoons butter

¼ cup all-purpose flour

2 cups light cream or half and half, heated

pinch paprika

2 tablespoons yellow mustard seeds, crushed with some warm water (see Notes)

salt to taste

Advance Preparation: The mustard seeds should be crushed in a mortar and pestle 20 minutes before using.

1. Melt the butter over low heat in a saucepan. Whisk in the flour and cook over low heat 2 minutes, being careful not to brown the flour.

2. Whisk in the warm cream and paprika. Bring to a boil over low heat, stirring occasionally. Lower the heat and simmer 2 minutes.

3. Add the crushed mustard seeds and adjust seasoning with salt. Serve at once.

Notes: First crush the dry mustard seeds a bit before adding a little water. The final consistency should be a thin paste. Two tablespoons of prepared mustard can replace the crushed mustard seeds.

Horseradish Sauce

Peberrodssauce

Horseradish is one of the few strong flavors appreciated in Denmark. The plant is related to cabbages and thrives over cold winters. Interestingly, the root itself has little pungency. The sharp flavors come about only after the root has been grated or cut, releasing enzymes that produce the aromatic qualities.

3 tablespoons butter

2 tablespoons all-purpose flour

1 cup light cream or half and half, heated

2 to 3 tablespoons grated fresh horseradish root (see Notes) or prepared horseradish

salt to taste

Advance Preparation: Bring the cream to a boil and remove from the heat.

1. Melt 2 tablespoons of the butter over low heat in a saucepan. Whisk in the flour and cook over low heat 2 minutes, being careful not to brown the flour.

2. Whisk in the warm cream and simmer over low heat 2 minutes.

3. Remove from heat. Stir in the horseradish. Stir in the remaining tablespoon of butter and adjust seasoning with salt. Serve at once.

Notes: Horseradish loses its potency soon after being exposed to air. Grate it immediately before using. Boiling the sauce after adding the grated horseradish turns it bitter.

Parsley Sauce

Persillesauce

Mild in flavor, parsley is the most widely used herb in the world. Flat-leaf (Italian) parsley has a more pronounced flavor and should be used when available. Chop some of the stems for an added boost in flavor.

2 tablespoons butter

2 tablespoons all-purpose flour

1 cup whole milk or light cream, heated

¼ cup minced flat-leaf parsley, some stems included

salt and pepper to taste

Advance Preparation: There is no advance preparation for this dish.

1. Melt the butter over low heat in a saucepan. Whisk in the flour and cook over low heat 2 minutes, being careful not to brown the flour.

2. Stir in the warm milk and bring to a boil over low heat. Lower the heat and simmer 2 minutes, stirring occasionally.

3. Add the chopped parsley and adjust seasoning with salt and pepper. Serve at once.

Notes: This sauce is delicious over any vegetable that goes well with a cream sauce and is an excellent accompaniment to poached fish.

Dill Sauce

Makes about
2 cups

Dildsauce

Dill is frequently used in Scandinavian cuisines, and in Denmark it can flavor a curing salmon or a poached breast of lamb. This sauce is excellent on vegetables and fish when you replace the stock with milk or cream.

---

2 tablespoons butter

2 tablespoons all-purpose flour

1½ cups rich stock, such as lamb or beef

¼ cup chopped fresh dill, stems included

1 tablespoon cider vinegar

½ tablespoon sugar

salt to taste

Advance Preparation: The stock should come from the cooking liquid of the meat with which this sauce will be served.

1. Melt the butter in a saucepan over low heat. Whisk in the flour and cook 2 minutes, being careful not to brown the flour.

2. Add the stock and whisk to combine. Heat to a boil and then lower the heat. Simmer 2 minutes, stirring occasionally.

3. Remove the sauce from the heat and stir in the dill, vinegar, and sugar. Allow to stand 1 minute. Adjust seasoning with salt and serve immediately.

Notes: For a richer sauce temper 1 egg yolk with some of the hot sauce and whisk into the sauce. Cook over very low heat, being careful not to boil the sauce.

132   **Part 1** Cooking Traditions

Mushroom Sauce

Champignonssauce

Earthy wild mushrooms, freshly gathered from the forest floor, always make a terrific accompaniment to game and meat dishes. This sauce is used extensively in Denmark to top fish, especially codfish mousse or fish patties.

6 tablespoons butter	½ cup heavy cream, heated
1 cup sliced assorted mushrooms	2 egg yolks
3 tablespoons all-purpose flour	salt to taste
1½ cups fish broth or stock, heated	

Advance Preparation: Clean the mushrooms with a dry cloth or brush. Do not soak or rinse them. Trim the stems and thinly slice them.

1. Melt the butter in a heavy saucepan over medium heat. Add the sliced mushrooms and sauté until they release their liquid and begin to brown, about 3 minutes.

2. Stir in the flour and cook an additional 2 minutes over low heat.

3. Whisk in the warm stock and then the cream. Bring to a boil over low heat. Lower the heat some more and simmer 2 minutes.

4. Whisk some of the hot sauce with the egg yolks and then whisk the tempered yolks into the sauce. Simmer 2 minutes, being careful not to allow the sauce to boil.

5. Adjust seasoning with salt and serve at once.

Notes: To accompany meats or game replace the fish stock with some cooking liquid from the meat, or use prepared beef stock.

Creamed Butter

Makes about
1 cup

Rørt Smør

The simplest of all "sauces" is creamed butter and the secret is in the beating. If beaten by hand, allow about 10 minutes of constant stirring. Using an electric mixer (on low speed) should take about 5 minutes. A little water can be added to help the process. Creamed butter is the basis for Danish compound butters, which have flavorings stirred in after creaming.

> ½ pound (2 sticks) unsalted quality butter, at room temperature
>
> a few drops of water, if using

1. Add the butter to a warm mixing bowl and beat using a low speed. Add a few drops of warm water, if necessary.

2. Continue to beat 5 minutes, until the butter is almost white in appearance. Use in any of the recipes below to make compound butters that can accompany a wide variety of vegetables, meat, and fish dishes.

Horseradish Butter (Peberrodssmør)

Excellent with roast beef, fried fish, and as a spread for *Smørrebrød*.

Add 2 tablespoons freshly grated horseradish to the recipe for Creamed Butter.

Anchovy Butter (Ansjossmør)

Great on steaks, grilled fish, and as a spread for *Smørrebrød*.

Mash 3 anchovy fillets with a fork until a paste forms. Add to the recipe for Creamed Butter.

Dill Butter (Dildsmør)

Perfect for smoked salmon, grilled fish, and as a spread for *Smørrebrød*.

Add 3 chopped hard-boiled egg yolks and ¼ cup chopped dill to the recipe for Creamed Butter.

Lemon Butter (Citronsmør)

A tasty addition to any fish dish or vegetable.

Add 2 tablespoons fresh lemon juice and 2 tablespoons chopped parsley to the recipe for Creamed Butter.

Drawn Butter Sauce

Smørsauce

Do not confuse this with the drawn butter (melted butter) served with crab claws and lobster tails. This roux-based sauce is meant for fish with a prominent flavor, rather than for mild-flavored fish or shellfish.

½ pound (2 sticks) butter, divided

4 tablespoons all-purpose flour

1 teaspoon paprika

2 cups cold water

salt to taste

Advance Preparation: There is no advance preparation for this dish.

1. Melt 1 stick of the butter in a saucepan over low heat. Whisk in the flour and paprika and cook over low heat 2 minutes, being careful not to brown the flour.

2. Whisk in the water and heat just to a boil. Lower the heat and simmer 2 minutes. Allow to cool until warm (don't let it get too cool or the butter added in the next step won't incorporate).

3. Slowly stir in the remaining 1 stick butter, in pieces, until they are absorbed. Adjust seasoning with salt and serve immediately.

Notes: The last addition of butter may be accomplished by swirling the pan, avoiding any stirring action with a utensil. This will improve texture.

Fruit Sauce

Frugtsauce

Fruit sauces, which rely on red fruit juices, are served with dessert puddings and custards.

---

2 cups cherry, raspberry, or plum juice

2 cups sugar

2 tablespoons cornstarch

pinch salt

Advance Preparation: There is no advance preparation for this dish.

1. Heat the fruit juice in a non-reactive saucepan. Stir in the sugar and cook over low heat to dissolve.

2. Make a slurry of the cornstarch with some water and stir it into the sweetened fruit juice. Heat to a boil and then remove from the heat.

3. Add a pinch of salt and serve over pudding or custard. This sauce may be served warm, at room temperature, or chilled.

Notes: A mixture of juices works well to balance the acidity and sweetness of various fruits.

Cinnamon Sauce

Kanelsauce

This sauce is used to top fruit salads, puddings, and pancakes. It is a very rich sauce, so use sparingly.

3 egg yolks
2 tablespoons sugar
½ tablespoon cornstarch
juice of 1 lemon

1 cup heavy cream, whipped firm
½ tablespoon cinnamon

Advance Preparation: All advance preparation may be found in the ingredient list.

1. Beat the egg yolks with the sugar until pale and fluffy.

2. Mix the cornstarch with 1 cup water and bring to a boil over medium heat, at which time it will be thickened and clear. Stir in the lemon juice.

3. Beat some of the hot sauce into the egg mixture to temper and then whisk this into the sauce. Cook 1 minute over low heat. Allow to cool thoroughly.

4. Fold the whipped cream into the cooled sauce and add the cinnamon. Refrigerate until needed.

Notes: A few gratings of nutmeg would be a tasty addition. A pinch of salt can be added to enhance flavor.

Cardamom Sauce

Makes about
1½ cups

Kardemommesauce

Cardamom is a spice normally associated with Indian and Middle Eastern cuisines. The Danes have recognized the flavorful interaction of cardamom with sweets and it is the most popular spice used in baking. Surprisingly, this sauce is meant for a savory roast beef dish.

¾ cup honey
½ teaspoon cardamom seeds,
    ground

½ cup port wine
pinch salt

Advance Preparation: If using whole cardamom seeds, they will need to be ground with a mortar and pestle.

1. In a small saucepan, mix the honey, ground cardamom, and ¼ cup water. Heat over low heat. Allow to simmer 5 minutes, stirring occasionally. Allow to cool.

2. When ready to serve add the port and salt. The thickness of the sauce may be adjusted with the amount of port wine added.

Notes: Bottled ready-to-use ground spices are always less flavorful than freshly ground. Use "decorticated" cardamom seeds for maximum flavor in this dish.

Smørrebrød

Smørrebrød are open sandwiches, artfully arranged with seemingly infinite combinations of meats, fish, vegetables, cheeses, and spreads. *Smørrebrød* are the soul food of Denmark. They are eaten for lunch, supper, with drinks, and as a late night snack. Chefs and homemakers alike take pride in a sandwich's eye appeal as well as in its taste. Contrasts are appreciated, and so the crunch of walnuts may play against the silkiness of a perfectly cooked egg, or the sweetness of beets with the bitter richness of liver paste.

With an endless combination of toppings, there are some guidelines to follow when constructing the perfect open sandwich. The base is a very thin slice of hearty dark rye bread, such as pumpernickel (although other varieties are used with more delicate toppings), that has been slathered quite liberally with sweet butter. Toppings must be generously applied, and no part of the buttered bread can be exposed. Keep in mind that *Smørrebrød* are eaten with a knife and fork, so these sandwiches are always served piled high. As important as flavor and quantity is presentation. The ingredients are arranged to be visually striking and colorful. When ordering for the first time in a restaurant in Copenhagen, one cannot go wrong with the "Trinity of *Smørrebrød*"—a herring sandwich followed by a meat selection, finishing with cheese.

Speculations as to the origin of the open sandwich abound. One popular account involves sausages and bread brought into the fields by workers for their noon meal. The modern version, with its extensive variations, came about in 1880s Copenhagen. Considered the father of modern *Smørrebrød*, Oskar Davidsen was a wine merchant who offered 178 varieties of open sandwiches, said to be a menu list of almost four feet in length! For those interested, the complete menu can be found at the end of this section.

Preparation

There are no formal recipes for *Smørrebrød*; rather suggestions are offered for toppings and combinations. The rest is left to the composer of these delights.

Base: Foremost, there must be a thin slice of generously buttered bread (after all, *Smørrebrød* means butter and bread), usually dark rye, but hearty white bread is sometimes used for delicate fish, especially shrimp.

Basics: These are added first to the buttered bread. Be sure to cover the entire surface, with no bread showing. A small piece of crisp lettuce is usually added to one side.

tiny shrimp	sliced hard-boiled eggs	roast beef
smoked salmon	scrambled eggs	raw beef (Tartar)
smoked oysters	assorted cheeses	grilled calves' liver
crabmeat	meatballs	roast pork
fried fish fillets	bacon	sardines

salami	lobster medallions	sliced ham
caviar	chicken salad	pickled herring tidbits
roast duck	fried eggs	liverwurst
raw egg yolk	beef brisket	

Garnishes/Toppings: Here is where your artistic eye comes into play. Think color combination as well as taste complement. Arrange these toppings to form interesting patterns; also play on textural differences.

tomato slices	lettuce	potato salad
sliced onion	coleslaw	radishes (sliced or roses)
fried onions	anchovies	meat jellies
marinated cucumbers	olives	remoulade
mayonnaise	pickles	pickled vegetables
parsley	dill	chives
horseradish	sliced new potatoes	sautéed mushrooms

For interesting and traditional Danish pairings, refer to Oskar Davidsen's original menu of 178 *Smørrebrød* offerings on the following pages. Feel free to use more familiar combinations, such as BLT, smoked salmon and cream cheese, or even roast beef with mashed potatoes and gravy!

Oskar Davidsen's 1888 *Smørrebrød* Menu

Superfine export caviar on toast

Shrimps

Shrimps, double portion (45-55)

"Rush Hour," shrimps double row (80-100)

Shrimps, pyramid portion (180-200)

Parboiled egg in mayonnaise, garnished with shrimps

Smoked salmon

Smoked salmon with raw egg yolk

Smoked salmon with scrambled egg

Smoked salmon with stewed mushrooms

Purée of smoked salmon with raw egg yolk, horseradish and onion

Lobster, freshly boiled

Lobster mayonnaise

Lobster with curry mayonnaise

Lobster with lettuce, sliced egg and mayonnaise

Lobster with asparagus in mayonnaise

¼ Lobster, chopped heart of lettuce and raw egg on toast

6 split crawfish tails with dill mayonnaise

Eel, freshly smoked, and scrambled egg

Eel, with scrambled egg, spinach and fried mushrooms
Fried fillet of plaice (flounder) and lemon
Fried fillet of plaice and remoulade
Dressed fried fillet of plaice
Fillet of plaice with deluxe garnish
Portuguese sardine in oil
Portuguese sardine and 2 boned anchovies in oyster sauce
Pickled herring "tidbits" with raw onion
Potato salad with pickled herring "tidbits" and seasoned beetroot
Pickled herring (Oskar Davidsen's special)
Fishcake and capers
Fishcake and remoulade
Freshly smoked herring
Freshly smoked herring with raw egg yolk
Freshly smoked herring, egg yolk and chopped radishes
Thinly sliced anchovies, beetroot, raw egg yolk, capers, onion and horseradish
4 boned anchovies in oyster sauce
4 boned anchovies with egg yolk and chives
4 boned anchovies with chopped egg and capers
4 boned anchovies with scrambled egg and chives
4 boned anchovies in oyster sauce, fried egg on toast
Swedish anchovy bird's-nest
Hot fried eel
Hot fried eel and remoulade
Cod roe, fried
Cod roe fried with remoulade
Cod roe, fried with 2 boned anchovies in oyster sauce
"Clipper Sandwich" – raw scraped beef, export caviar and smoked salmon
"Hans Andersen's Favorite" – bacon, tomato, liver paste with truffles, meat jelly, horseradish
Rare, minced beef with capers and onions and fried egg
Boeuf Tartar (scraped raw beef)
Boeuf Tartar with pickles
"Strip Tease" – scraped beef with raw egg yolk
Scraped raw meat, shrimps, parboiled egg and fresh lettuce
"Union Jack" sandwich – raw scraped fillet of beef with shrimps and raw egg yolk
Boeuf Tartar with 2 boned anchovies in oyster sauce, egg yolk and chopped onions or chives
Raw scraped meat, export caviar and 2 Limfjord oysters flanked by 2 rows of shrimps
Roast beef with tomato and cucumber salad
Roast beef with crisp bacon and onions

Roast beef with cold Béarnaise sauce

Roast beef with superfine export caviar

Roast beef and horseradish

Roast beef and remoulade

Roast beef with potato salad and chives

Fried calves' liver and onions

Fried calves' liver with fried egg

Fried calves' liver with cucumber salad

Fried calves' liver with bacon and mushrooms

Fried calves' liver with bacon and onions

Slices of juicy steak, parboiled egg, crisp onions, and sliced tomato on sour bread or toast

Steak and fried onions

Steak with fried egg

Roast duck with red cabbage and cucumber salad

Brisket of beef, freshly boiled, and horseradish

Brisket of beef and pickles

Brisket of beef and remoulade

Brisket of beef with tomato and 2 anchovies

Roast chicken with cucumber and tomato

Roast pork with meat jelly and smoked ham

½ young pigeon and stewed mushrooms

Liver paste with truffles, 2 anchovies in oyster sauce and fried egg

Liver paste with cucumber salad

Liver paste with thin slices of crisp bacon and stewed mushrooms

Liver paste with spiced lard, meat jelly and thinly sliced, juicy salt veal (the "Vet's Supper")

Liver paste with 2 boned anchovies in oyster sauce and grated horseradish

Liver paste with Russian herring salad

Liver paste, sliced tomato and cucumber salad

Lamb's liver, fried tomato and mushrooms

Fried forcemeat cakes with red cabbage, meat jelly and beetroot

Fried forcemeat cakes and cucumber salad

Fried forcemeat cakes with meat jelly and thinly sliced, juicy salt veal

Fried forcemeat cakes and cucumber salad

Fried forcemeat cakes with meat jelly and thinly sliced, juicy salt veal

Ham, sliced egg and meat jelly

Freshly boiled, mild-cured ham and meat jelly

Ham and scrambled eggs

Ham with Camembert, raw egg yolk and chives

Ham with chicken salad

Ham with Bombay curry salad

Ham with vegetable salad

Ham with fried egg

Ham with fried calves' kidney and remoulade

Ham with bird's liver and fried egg

Ham with homemade goose liver paste, Madeira jelly

Bayonne ham, roast beef and meat jelly

Crisp bacon and fried egg

Crisp bacon with tomato and Camembert cheese

Crisp bacon with fried onions

Crisp bacon with creamed mushrooms

Juicy, tender, salt veal and meat jelly

Freshly boiled tongue with meat jelly

Tongue with Italian salad

Tongue with fried egg

Tongue with homemade goose liver paste

Tongue with sliced egg and meat jelly

Homemade collared pork

As above with spiced lard and meat jelly

Corned brisket of beef with horseradish

As above with spiced lard and meat jelly

As above with potato salad and chives

Salami sausage, liver paste and meat jelly (the "Vet's Breakfast")

Salami with raw egg yolk, grated horseradish and chopped chives

Salami sausage with meat jelly

Salami with scrambled eggs and chives

Salami and fried egg on toast

Salami with spiced lard, sliced potato and chives

Luncheon sausage with meat jelly

Italian salad

"Bombay Toast" – macaroni, chicken, giblets in curry mayonnaise with egg and smoked salmon

Russian herring salad

Russian herring salad with egg

Vegetable salad

Curry salad

Hot scrambled eggs with smoked salmon on toast

Hot scrambled eggs, 4 boned anchovies in oyster sauce and chopped chives on toast

Hot scrambled eggs and fried mushrooms on toast

Parboiled egg with shrimps

Parboiled egg with remoulade

Parboiled egg with export caviar

Parboiled egg with smoked eel

Parboiled egg and meat jelly

Parboiled egg with Russian herring salad

Parboiled egg and herring "tidbits"

Parboiled egg and boned anchovies in oyster sauce

Parboiled egg and pickles

Parboiled egg with tomato and 2 boned anchovies in oyster sauce

Parboiled egg with tomato and fried onions

Parboiled egg with cheese mayonnaise and chopped radishes

Poached egg on toast with stewed mushrooms and fresh lobster

Parboiled egg, tomato and horseradish

Sliced tomato, scrambled egg, boned anchovies in oyster sauce and chives

Tomato and horseradish

Tomato with scrambled eggs and chives

Tomato and 2 boned anchovies in oyster sauce

Tomato and fried onions

Tomato with cheese mayonnaise

Tomato, fried onions and fried egg

Tomato, scrambled egg, 2 boned anchovies in oyster sauce and chopped chives, on toast

Tomato, raw egg yolk, capers, horseradish and raw onion

Grated carrot with raw egg yolk and sliced lemon

Camembert with thin, juicy slices of salt veal and meat jelly

Swiss cheese

Samsø

Maribo

Olde Holsteiner cheese with butter or spiced lard

Olde Holsteiner cheese with red currant jelly

Smoked cheese with fresh cucumber and paprika

Christian IX cheese

Danish blue cheese

Danish blue cheese with raw egg yolk

Smoked cheese with raw egg yolk and chives

Potkäse cheese

Potkäse with raw egg yolk and chopped radishes

Camembert

Camembert with 2 boned anchovies in oyster sauce

Brie

1 slice bread with butter or dripping

Part 2

Baking
Traditions

Breads

Danish bread baking produces very hearty loaves that store well. Many are based on rye grain, which does not have the gluten proteins required for airy breads porous with fermentation gases. *Rugbrød* is the bread used most often in *Smørrebrød* (page 139). The dense loaves can be sliced very thin, providing a firm but non-intrusive base to the true stars of the sandwich—the toppings. Bread becomes more nutritious and dense with the addition of sunflower seeds, rolled oats, or whole rye grain. In addition to being used for *Smørrebrød*, bread is served at most meals and is often mentioned in recipes as a standard accompaniment to the dish—with butter generously applied.

Danish Rye Bread (Rugbrød)

Grading Bread (Sigtebrød)

Old-Fashioned Danish Black Bread (Gammelsurbrød)

Sourdough Bread (Surbrød)

Potato Bread (Kartoffelbrød)

Cheese Bread (Ostebrød)

Beer Bread (Øllebrød)

Buttermilk Quick Bread (Kærnemælksbrod)

Oatmeal Griddle Bread (Knækkerbrød)

Flatbread (Fladbrød)

Almond Bread (Mandelbrød)

Rusks (Skorpor)

Danish Rye Bread

Rugbrød

This is the traditional sandwich bread that is sliced thin, slathered with rich creamery butter, and then topped with an assortment of meats, fish, cheeses, and garnishes. The recipe produces a dense dough that does not rise as much as wheat dough.

1 tablespoon dry yeast	2 tablespoons molasses
½ cup very warm water (105 to 110 degrees F)	3 cups rye flour, preferably stone-ground
1½ cups buttermilk, heated to 110 degrees F	about 1 cup whole wheat flour

Advance Preparation: Slowly heat the buttermilk to about 110 degrees F. Heat the oven to 350 degrees F at least one hour before baking.

1. Sprinkle the yeast over the warm water and allow to stand without mixing until the yeast dissolves, about 3 minutes.

2. Stir the dissolved yeast and molasses into the warm buttermilk and add this to a warmed mixing bowl of an electric mixer. Begin to stir with a paddle attachment.

3. Slowly add the rye flour, about ½ cup at a time, allowing the flour to be absorbed before adding another portion.

4. Switch to a dough hook and add the whole wheat flour, a little at a time, until a smooth, workable dough forms, using more or less wheat flour as required. Knead 3 minutes.

5. Remove the dough hook and cover the bowl with a damp cloth. Place it in a draft-free, warm area and allow dough to ferment and rise 2 hours.

6. Punch down the dough and place in a 9-inch loaf pan. Cover and allow to rise 1 hour in a warm area.

7. Bake for 1 hour, or until the bread sounds hollow when tapped and the top springs back to the touch. Allow to cool on a wire rack.

Notes: Sunflower seeds or whole rye grain may be added to the dough. Use ⅓ cup. For a darker loaf, 1 tablespoon of caramel powder or instant espresso coffee powder may be added to the rye flour.

Grading Bread

Sigtebrød

Grading bread is a rye bread made with more wheat flour than rye. Its name comes from the grading of flour, and in this bread, coarse milling is required for an authentic loaf but stone-ground rye flour should suffice.

1 tablespoon dry yeast	2 cups stone-ground rye flour
2½ cups very warm water (105 to 110 degrees F)	about 6 cups whole wheat flour
3 tablespoons butter, melted	1 teaspoon salt
½ cup plain yogurt	

Advance Preparation: Heat the oven to 350 degrees F at least one hour before baking.

1. Sprinkle the yeast over ½ cup of the very warm water. Allow to dissolve and sink to the bottom, about 3 minutes. Stir to form a creamy mixture.

2. Mix the dissolved yeast with the remaining 2 cups of very warm water, the melted butter, and yogurt. Place in the warmed bowl of an electric mixer.

3. Slowly add the rye flour, using the paddle attachment to the electric mixer. Stir 2 minutes.

4. Gradually add the whole wheat flour, 1 cup at a time, allowing the flour to absorb the liquid before adding more flour, using just enough to form a smooth, elastic dough that is not sticky or too dry. Add the salt.

5. Switch to a dough hook and knead the dough for 5 minutes. Cover with a damp cloth and allow to rise for 2 hours in a draft-free area.

6. Punch the dough down and shape into 2 round loaves. Allow the loaves to rise 1½ hours, or until doubled in bulk.

7. Bake for 30 to 40 minutes, or until the loaves sound hollow when tapped. Allow to cool on wire racks.

Notes: One teaspoon of caraway seeds may be added. In some regions *sigtebrød* includes spices such as cloves or cardamom.

Old-Fashioned Danish Black Bread

Gammelsurbrød

This pumpernickel-style bread uses a sour rye starter made the day before. As with most Danish breads, this loaf is made to be sliced very thin and eaten with ample quantities of sweet creamery butter.

---

1 tablespoon dry yeast

2 cups very warm water (105 to 110 degrees F)

3 or more cups stone-ground coarse rye flour

1 teaspoon salt

about 1 cup whole wheat flour

Advance Preparation: Sprinkle the yeast over the 2 cups very warm water. When the yeast sinks, stir to form a creamy mixture. Stir in 2 cups of rye flour to form a smooth paste. Cover and allow to stand at room temperature overnight (this is the starter).

1. Beat the starter and stir in the salt. Mix in 1 cup rye flour and 1 cup wheat flour. Beat the mixture for 3 minutes. Cover and allow to rise 2 hours.

2. Turn the dough onto a surface dusted with a little rye and wheat flour. Knead for 5 minutes, adding additional flours to form a smooth dough that is not sticky.

3. Divide the dough in two and place each half into a 9-inch loaf pan. Cover and allow to rise until doubled in bulk, about 2 hours. Heat the oven to 300 degrees F.

4. Bake the bread for 1 to 1½ hours, until the top is firm and the bread sounds hollow when tapped. Cool on wire racks.

Notes: A pan of water may be placed in the oven on a rack below the bread to prevent the bottoms from getting too hard. To make the bread very dark, 1 tablespoon of caramel powder or instant espresso powder can be added to the flours.

Sourdough Bread

Makes 1 loaf plus additional starter

Surbrød

Making sourdough bread requires a sour starter, which can be made several days in advance. Once formed, the starter can be maintained indefinitely (see Notes).

Starter:
1 tablespoon dry yeast
1 cup very warm water (105 to 110 degrees F)
1 teaspoon sugar
2 cups bread flour

Bread:
½ cup milk
2 tablespoons sugar
1 tablespoon butter
3 to 3½ cups all-purpose flour

Advance Preparation: Make the starter 3 days in advance of baking bread. Sprinkle the yeast over the 1 cup very warm water. Allow to dissolve and sink to the bottom of the bowl. Stir to form a creamy mixture. Blend in the sugar and 2 cups bread flour to form a smooth paste. Cover with a cloth and allow to ferment for 3 days at room temperature, stirring once each day.

1. Bring the milk with the sugar and butter just to a boil. Remove from the heat and allow to cool to lukewarm.

2. Measure 1 cup of starter and stir it into the milk mixture and place in the bowl of an electric mixer. Slowly mix in 2 cups of flour, ½ cup at a time, using the paddle attachment of the electric mixer. Switch to a dough hook and continue to add flour. Use enough flour to form a smooth, soft dough that does not stick to the hands.

3. Knead the dough for 5 minutes using the mixer. Turn the dough onto a floured surface and knead by hand for 2 minutes. Place it in a bowl and cover with a cloth. Allow to rise for 2 hours in a warm, draft-free area.

4. Punch the dough down and allow it to rise again, covered, until doubled in bulk, about 1 hour.

5. Heat the oven to 400 degrees F. Place the dough in a 9-inch loaf pan and cover with a cloth. Allow to rise once more in the pan, until doubled in bulk, about 1 hour.

6. Bake about 1 hour, or until the bread sounds hollow when tapped and the crust is golden brown. Cool on a wire rack.

Notes: The starter can be kept indefinitely in the refrigerator, if properly fed. To the remaining starter from this recipe, add 1 cup of warm water, ½ cup flour, and 1 teaspoon sugar. Stir to combine and refrigerate until needed. Repeat this process as starter is consumed.

Potato Bread

Makes 1 loaf

Kartoffelbrød

Leftover potatoes can turn an ordinary bread recipe into one that is hearty without being too dense.

½ cup mashed potatoes (see Notes)

4 tablespoons butter, at room temperature

¼ cup sugar

1 egg

1 tablespoon dry yeast

½ cup very warm water (105 to 110 degrees F)

½ teaspoon salt

½ cup milk, scalded and then cooled to lukewarm

about 4 cups all-purpose flour

melted butter

Advance Preparation: Cook the potato, if no leftovers are available.

1. Cream the butter with the sugar until blended. Add the potatoes and beat in the egg to form a smooth mixture.

2. Sprinkle the yeast over the ½ cup very warm water and allow to stand 2 minutes. Stir to incorporate.

3. Whisk the dissolved yeast into the butter mixture. Add the salt and scalded milk. Stir to combine. Pour into the mixing bowl of an electric mixer.

4. Using the paddle attachment of the electric mixer, add 3 cups of flour, 1 cup at a time, allowing each addition to be absorbed before adding more.

5. Switch to a dough hook and add enough additional flour to form a smooth, stiff dough that does not stick to the hands. Knead 5 minutes.

6. Turn the dough onto a floured surface and knead by hand 2 minutes. Place the dough in a bowl and cover with a cloth. Allow to rise 2 hours in a warm, draft-free area.

7. Punch the dough down and place it in a 9-inch loaf pan. Cover and allow to rise until doubled in bulk, about 1½ hours. Heat the oven to 375 degrees F.

8. Brush the top of the bread with melted butter and bake for 1 hour or until the top is golden and the bread sounds hollow when tapped. Cool on a wire rack.

Notes: Instant potato flakes may replace fresh potatoes. Prepare according to label directions. Mashed sweet potatoes make an excellent substitute *(Sødt Kartoffelbrød)*. If cooking raw potatoes for this bread, save 1 cup of the cooking liquid to dissolve the yeast.

Cheese Bread

Ostebrød

Sharp-flavored cheeses, such as aged cheddar, work best in bread dough. Cheese bread is delicious as an accompaniment to soup, making it a filling meal, and provides great flavor to almost any sandwich.

½ cup milk	½ cup very warm water (105 to 110 degrees F)
2 tablespoons sugar	about 3 cups all-purpose flour
½ teaspoon salt	1 cup grated sharp cheese, such as cheddar
1 tablespoon dry yeast	

Advance Preparation: There is no advance preparation for this dish.

1. Bring the milk with the sugar and salt just to a boil. Remove from the heat and allow to cool to lukewarm.

2. Sprinkle the yeast over the ½ cup warm water and allow to stand 2 minutes. Stir to dissolve.

3. Mix the dissolved yeast with the milk mixture and pour into the mixing bowl of an electric mixer. Using the paddle attachment of the electric mixer, gradually stir in 2 cups of flour to form a smooth paste. Stir in the grated cheese.

4. Switch to a dough hook and continue to add enough flour to form a soft, smooth dough that does not stick to the hands. Knead 5 minutes.

5. Turn the dough onto a floured surface and knead by hand 2 minutes. Place in a bowl and cover. Allow to rise in a warm, draft-free area for 2 hours.

6. Punch the dough down and place in a 9-inch loaf pan. Cover and allow to rise until double in bulk, about 1½ hours. Heat the oven to 375 degrees F.

7. Bake for 1 hour, or until the top is golden and the bread sounds hollow when tapped. Cool on a wire rack.

Notes: Some "daring" Danish bakers and chefs are adding chopped jalapeños to this dough. Use 2 tablespoons for this recipe. The heat of the jalapeño can be controlled by removing the white membrane and seeds contained within.

Beer Bread

Øllebrød

The Egyptians are generally credited with discovering beer-brewing and bread-making. It seems only natural that beer would make a complementary addition to the liquids used in making bread. The Danes are great bread bakers and aficionados of finely crafted beer, making this a foreseen combination.

¾ cup beer (see Notes)	1 teaspoon salt
¼ cup molasses	2 cups stone-ground rye flour
1 tablespoon dry yeast	about 2 cups whole wheat flour
¼ cup very warm water (105 to 110 degrees F)	

Advance Preparation: Open the beer and allow to come to room temperature before using.

1. Mix 1 cup water, the beer, and molasses together in a small saucepan. Heat the mixture to lukewarm.

2. Sprinkle the yeast over the ¼ cup very warm water and allow to stand 2 minutes. Stir to dissolve. Add the salt and stir this into the beer mixture. Pour the mixture into the bowl of an electric mixer.

3. Stir in the rye flour using the paddle attachment of the electric mixer. Add 1 cup wheat flour and stir to form a smooth batter.

4. Switch to a dough hook and add additional wheat flour until a smooth dough forms that does not stick to the hands. Knead 5 minutes.

5. Turn the dough onto a floured surface and knead by hand 2 minutes. Place in a bowl and cover with a cloth. Allow to rise 2 hours in a warm, draft-free area.

6. Punch the dough down and shape it into a round loaf on a baking sheet. Allow to rise until doubled in bulk, about 1 hour. Heat the oven to 400 degrees F.

7. Bake for 10 minutes. Lower the heat to 325 degrees F and continue to bake an additional 50 minutes, or until the bread sounds hollow when tapped. Cool on a wire rack.

Notes: Dark beers provide more flavor than pilsner-style beer in this recipe.

Buttermilk Quick Bread

Kærnemælksbrød

Denmark produces some of the world's finest butter, and the liquid leftover after churning is called buttermilk. It adds richness to the dough and brightness to the taste of the bread.

---

1 tablespoon baking powder

1 tablespoon baking soda

½ teaspoon salt

1½ cups all-purpose flour

3 cups whole wheat flour

2 tablespoons brown sugar

2 eggs

2 tablespoons butter, melted

3 cups buttermilk

Advance Preparation: Heat the oven to 325 degrees F.

1. Sift the baking powder, baking soda, salt, and all-purpose flour together. Toss in the whole wheat flour with the brown sugar and mix briefly.

2. In a separate bowl, whisk the eggs, melted butter, and buttermilk. Stir the dry ingredients into the buttermilk mixture to form a smooth batter.

3. Pour the batter into 2 9-inch loaf pans and bake for 1 hour or until a tester comes out clean from the center of the bread and the top springs back when pressed. Allow to cool on wire racks.

Notes: For a more substantial bread *(Kærnemælksbrød med Nødder)*, add 1 cup of chopped walnuts to the batter, increase the brown sugar to ½ cup, and add 1 teaspoon cinnamon and ½ teaspoon nutmeg to the dry ingredients when sifting.

Oatmeal Griddle Bread

Knækkerbrød

Quick breads rely on chemical leavenings to make their product light and airy. They are, as their name implies, easy to prepare with no need for long rising times. Rather than being baked, this bread is cooked on a griddle.

3 cups rolled oats, ground	1 pound butter, melted and cooled
3 cups all-purpose flour	1½ cups buttermilk
1 teaspoon baking soda	
1 teaspoon salt	

Advance Preparation: Using a food processor, pulse the oats until finely ground. Prepare a griddle for cooking.

1. Mix the ground oats with the flour, baking soda, and salt.

2. Mix the melted butter with the buttermilk. Combine the dry ingredients with the buttermilk mixture to form a smooth, stiff dough that can be rolled out.

3. Divide the dough into 6 pieces. Roll out each portion on a floured surface to a round shape with a thickness of ½-inch.

4. Cook breads on a well-greased, non-stick griddle over medium heat. When golden brown on the first side, turn (only once) and cook the other side until browned.

Notes: Oat flour is available in some upscale and organic markets, and can be used to replace the ground oats. Measure 2½ cups if using oat flour.

Flatbread

Fladbrød

Flatbreads are quite common across Scandinavia and are often crisp and dry, meant for long-term storage. This bread is crisp on the edges, but relatively soft, more like a Mediterranean flatbread. Modern Danish chefs are using *fladbrød* as a base for wraps, filling them with interesting combinations such as goat cheese, leeks, and herbs.

2 cups stone ground whole wheat flour	½ teaspoon baking soda
1 cup graham flour (see Notes)	½ teaspoon salt
1 tablespoon sugar	½ cup buttermilk, warmed
1 teaspoon baking powder	½ cup hot water
	4 tablespoons butter, melted

Advance Preparation: Prepare a heavy, non-stick griddle for cooking.

1. Mix the whole wheat flour with the graham flour, sugar, baking powder, baking soda, and salt.

2. Mix the buttermilk, hot water, and melted butter. Stir the dry ingredients into the liquids to form a smooth, firm dough.

3. Divide the dough into 6 pieces and roll each out on a floured surface, forming thin rounds 8 to 10 inches in diameter.

4. Cook each flatbread on a well-greased griddle over high heat. When the edges are crisp and brown, flip and cook briefly on the other side. Do not stack the breads when cooling.

Notes: If graham flour is not available, mix ⅔ cup all-purpose flour with a scant ⅔ cup wheat bran and ½ tablespoon wheat germ for each cup of graham flour needed.

Almond Bread

Mandelbrød

There are fewer boundaries in Scandinavian baking. Breads and cakes are inter-changeable terms, and Danish quick breads can be quite sweet and filling.

½ cup chopped almonds	1½ cups all-purpose flour
3 eggs	2 teaspoons baking powder
½ cup sugar	½ teaspoon salt

Advance Preparation: Warm a heavy skillet over medium heat. Add the chopped almonds and stir them constantly until aromatic and lightly browned. Allow to cool. Heat the oven to 375 degrees F.

1. Beat the eggs with the sugar until pale and thick, about 2 minutes.

2. Sift the flour with the baking powder and salt. Stir this into the egg mixture to form a smooth batter.

3. Mix in the toasted almonds and place in a 9-inch loaf pan. Bake for 45 minutes or until set in the center to the touch. Allow to cool on a wire rack.

Notes: A sugar glaze or frosting makes a delicious addition to this cake-style bread. Mix 1½ cups sifted powdered sugar with 2 tablespoons softened butter, ½ teaspoon vanilla extract, 3 tablespoons heavy cream, and a pinch of salt to form a smooth and creamy frosting.

Rusks

Skorpor

Skorpor means crust. Rusks are twice-cooked bread slices that were originally meant for long-term storage at sea. This technique, which produces very hard, crisp biscuits, is also seen in Italian *biscotti* and German *zwieback*. Both terms translate as "twice-baked."

2 cups all-purpose flour	5 tablespoons butter, softened
2 teaspoons baking powder	1 beaten egg
½ teaspoon salt	⅓ cup sour cream

Advance Preparation: Heat the oven to 450 degrees F.

1. Sift the flour with the baking powder and salt. Gently cut in the soft butter, being careful not to cream the butter or form a paste. The mixture should resemble coarse meal.

2. Mix the beaten egg with the sour cream and add this to the flour mixture in portions, forming a moist, soft dough.

3. Form the dough into a 2-inch-wide cylinder and slice into ¾-inch-long pieces. Place the rusks on a baking sheet and bake until golden and airy, about 15 minutes. Shut off the oven.

4. Cut each rusk in half and separate them. Return the rusks to the oven to dry out, leaving the oven door partially open.

Notes: The rusks are very crisp, therefore serve with tea, coffee, or other beverages. Rusks can form a sturdy base for creamed stews and go well with piping-hot soup.

Desserts and Sweets

Scandinavia is home to masters of the baking arts and nowhere is this more evident than in Denmark, home of "Danish Pastry," which interestingly is called *wienerbrød* (Viennese bread) across Scandinavia. Throughout Denmark's history, its royalty would employ highly trained chefs and bakers from Austria and surrounding areas. It was these chefs who developed the quintessential baked goods of Denmark, thus the name. *Wienerbrød* became known as Danish pastry around 1915 in America when it was popularized by L.C. Klitteng who founded the Danish Culinary Studio in New York City. It is said that he baked these pastries for President Wilson's wedding and then went on a tour, demonstrating and baking his way across the U.S. Formed into attractive shapes and filled with an endless variety of jams, nuts, and custards, Danish pastry is the culmination of the baking arts. Light and flaky, it is made in the same way as puff pastry. For Danish pastry, butter is encased in yeast dough (a short dough is used for puff paste) and is then rolled out, folded, turned, and re-rolled. This process is repeated several times, creating hundreds of layers of buttery dough that puffs up when baked.

Cakes and tortes abound as do delicate cookies. Almonds and marzipan are common flavor additions to all. Although pies are not commonly found in Denmark, berries and fruits are often included in cakes, tarts, and rich puddings made from exquisitely fresh dairy products. While savory recipes seem to lack spices and strong herbs, Danish sweet baked goods often include significant amounts of cardamom, cinnamon, cloves, and saffron. Needless to say, superior quality butter makes its way into many of Denmark's baked treats along with thick sour cream, buttermilk, and rich whole milk.

Danish Pastries (Wienerbrød)

Pastry Twists (Klejner)

Kringle (Coffee Bread) (Kringle)

Butter Pastry (Butterdejg)

Butter Horns (Smørhorn)

Quick Coffee Bread (Gallop Kringle)

Danish Doughnuts (Æbleskiver)

Cornets with Whipped Cream (Kræmmerhuse med Flødeskum)

Apple Cake (Æblekage)

Danish Layer Cake (Dansk Lagkage)

Sour Cream Cake (Sur Fløde Kage)

Sand Cake (Sandkage)

Seven Sisters' Cake (Søsterkage)

Butter Cake (Smørkage)

Othello Cake (Othello Lagkage)

Sour Cream Coffee Cake (Sur Fløde Kaffeekage)

Tosca Torte (Toscatærte)

Cardamom Cake (Kardemommenkage)

Almond Cake (Mandelkage)

Sour Cream Chocolate Cake (Chokoladekiksekage)

Poppy Seed Cake (Valmuefrøkage)

Applesauce Cake (Æblesaucekage)

Whipped Cream Cake (Flødekage)

Gingerbread (Ingefærkage)

Marzipan Cakes (Kransekager)

Jewish Cakes (Jødekager)

Danish Short Bread (Finsk Brød)

Sour Cream Cookies (Sur Fløde Kager)

Almond Rings (Mandel Kranse)

Brown Cookies (Brunkager)

Sugar Cookies (Sukker Smaakager)

Peppernuts (Pebernødder)

Anise Cookies (Aniskager)

Cardamom Cookies (Kardemommekager)

Caraway Cookies (Kommenkager)

Copenhagen Cookies (Københavnerkager)

Hazelnut Cookies (Hasselnødkager)

Vanilla Rings (Vaniljekranse)

Danish Toast (Arme Riddere)

"Veiled Country Lass" (Bondepige med Slør)

Rice Fritters (Risengrynsklatter)

Thin Pancakes (Tynde Pandekager)

Red Fruit Pudding (Rødgrød med Fløde)

Christmas Rice Pudding (Julerisengrød)

Applesauce (Æblegrød)

Danish Pastries

Makes about 2½ pounds of dough

Wienerbrød

This versatile dough can be made into a variety of shapes and filled with endless goodies. With a little practice and patience, rich, flaky pastries can be produced from even the most modest kitchen. This dough stores well in the freezer, tightly sealed.

---

2 tablespoons dry yeast

1 cup milk, scalded and then cooled to lukewarm

½ cup sugar

2 eggs

5 cups all-purpose flour

1 pound (4 sticks) cold unsalted butter or margarine (see Notes)

Favorite filling (jams, custard, soft cheese, etc.)

Advance Preparation: Dissolve the yeast in the warm milk. Stir in the sugar and eggs. Sift in the flour and mix to form a smooth dough. Knead the dough for several minutes by hand. Refrigerate 1 hour.

1. Roll the dough out to a square about ¼-inch thick. Place the butter between sheets of plastic wrap and pound it until pliable but not soft. Roll it into a square 2-inches smaller than the dough. The dough and butter should be of similar consistency.

2. Place the butter on the dough and encase it with the dough by bringing the corner points to the center. Seal the butter in by pinching the dough at the seams.

3. Roll this dough out carefully to ½-inch thickness. Fold in thirds as for a letter. Turn the dough 90 degrees and roll it out again to ½-inch thickness. Fold in thirds and refrigerate for 30 minutes. Repeat this entire process two more times, refrigerating between "turns." Refrigerate the dough until thoroughly chilled before use.

To make pastries: Roll the dough out to a thickness of ½-inch. Trim the edges with a very sharp knife. Two common shapes are made in the following ways:

PINWHEELS: Cut the rolled and trimmed dough into 4-inch squares. Starting 1-inch from the center, make straight cuts to the corners of the squares. Press alternate cut corners into the center of each square, forming pinwheels. Add a dollop of your favorite filling (jam, custard, cheese) to the center.

BEAR CLAWS: Cut the trimmed pastry into 2-inch by 4-inch rectangles. Place filling on one half of each rectangle, lengthwise. Fold the opposite edges over the filling to form long narrow rectangles. Pinch the seams closed. Make 4 evenly spaced parallel cuts across the width of each pastry, stopping ½-inch from the seam edge. Bend the pastries into a curve so that the parallel cuts open up.

(continued on next page)

Danish Pastries *(continued)*

Cover and allow the formed pinwheel or bear claw pastries to rise until doubled in bulk. Bake at 400 degrees F for 8 to 10 minutes or until flaky and golden brown. An egg wash or sugar glaze may be added before baking.

Notes: It is said that margarine makes a flakier product, but significant flavor is lost with its use. Consider using a mixture of half butter and half margarine, creamed together first and then chilled before using.

Danish pastry is not Danish after all. A hint to its origin can be gleaned from its Danish name, *Weienerbrød,* or Viennese bread. The Austrians have been considered the finest of European bakers for many years and so Danish aristocracy would employ Viennese bakers in their kitchens. A strike by Danish bakers in the 1850s resulted in hiring of foreign bakers to fill the niche. Many from Austria took these jobs and introduced their style of specialty breads and pastries to Danes of all social status. It is said that the Danish contribution was to increase the number of eggs in the Viennese pastry recipes. This history is certified by the Danish Confectioners, Bakers and Chocolate Makers Associations.

Pastry Twists

Klejner

These delightful doughnuts are deep-fried and are most often eaten during Christmas. When properly drained after frying, they will keep well in a cookie tin. A special cutter, called a *Fattigman* or *klejner cutter,* is sold to make these treats.

8 tablespoons unsalted butter, at room temperature	3½ cups all-purpose flour
1 cup sugar	2 teaspoons baking powder
3 eggs	1 teaspoon ground cardamom
¼ cup heavy cream	½ teaspoon salt

Advance Preparation: Prepare a frying area with paper towels to drain the twists. Begin to heat a light cooking oil in a wide pot to 365 degrees F.

1. Beat the butter with the sugar until light in color and fluffy. Beat in the eggs, one at a time. Add the cream and whisk to form a smooth mixture.

2. Sift the flour with the baking powder, cardamom, and salt.

3. Mix the dry ingredients with the butter mixture to form a smooth, soft dough.

4. Roll the dough to ¼-inch thickness. Cut into narrow diamond shapes about 3 inches across. Make a slit in the center of each diamond and pull one point of the diamond partially through the slit.

5. Fry the pastries in the hot oil until golden brown, turning once. Remove the twists to paper towels to drain thoroughly. Allow to cool completely and then store in a cookie tin or jar.

Notes: Danes use a long knitting needle to turn and remove the twists from the hot oil. A dusting of powdered sugar just before serving is a nice addition to these holiday treats.

Kringle (Coffee Bread)

Kringle

Kringle (pronounced *kring-leh*) are pretzel-shaped, filled coffee cakes made in a similar way to Danish pastries. Flaky layers of pastry are created by successively rolling and folding butter-encased yeast dough. The symbol for a bakery in Denmark, and appearing on every baker's outdoor sign, is the image of a pretzel, representing a kringle.

---

1 cup raisins

½ pound (2 sticks) unsalted butter,
    at room temperature

1 teaspoon cardamom

1 tablespoon dry yeast

1 cup milk, scalded and then cooled
    to lukewarm

3½ cups all-purpose flour

1 egg

¾ cup sugar plus more for dusting

1 egg yolk

2 tablespoons cream

Advance Preparation: Plump the raisins by simmering them in water for 5 minutes. Drain and add 4 tablespoons of the butter. Stir and allow to cool. Mix in the cardamom and reserve the filling until needed.

1. Sprinkle the yeast over ¼ cup of the scalded warm milk. Allow to stand 5 minutes and then stir to form a creamy mixture.

2. Cream the remaining 1½ sticks unsalted butter with ½ cup of the flour to form a paste. Reserve.

3. Beat the egg with the sugar and remaining ¾ cup scalded warm milk. Add the yeast mixture. Stir in the remaining 3 cups flour to form a smooth dough that can be rolled out.

4. Roll out the dough on a floured surface to form a rectangle about ½-inch thick. Spread the reserved butter and flour paste across the surface stopping about ½-inch from the edges.

5. Fold the dough in half, pinching the seams closed. Gently roll the dough to twice its size. Fold into thirds, as for a letter. Roll out to ½-inch thickness. Turn 90 degrees, fold in thirds and roll out again. Fold in thirds and refrigerate the dough, wrapped in plastic film, for 1 hour.

6. Roll, fold, and turn the dough 2 more times. Wrap in plastic film and refrigerate 1 more hour.

7. Roll the dough out to a long rectangle approximately 8-inch x 20-inch. Spread the raisin filling across the surface of the dough and roll up jelly-roll fashion. Pinch the ends tightly to seal.

8. Bend the pastry into a pretzel shape and flatten it to about ½-inch thickness. Cover with a damp towel and allow the kringle to rise in a warm, draft-free area for 1 hour, or until nicely risen. Meanwhile heat the oven to 350 degrees F.

9. Beat the egg yolk with the cream and brush the surface of the pastry with this mixture. Sprinkle sugar over and bake for 30 minutes, or until golden brown. Cool on a wire rack.

Notes: Ground almonds mixed with sugar is often used to garnish a kringle. Cinnamon can replace the cardamom or a mixture of the spices may be used in the filling. Consider other fillings such as sweetened cheese or cherry preserves.

Butter Pastry

Butterdejg

This versatile dough may be used for savory dishes, such as a shell for creamed chicken, as well as for fruit tarts, pretzel-shaped cookies dusted with sugar, and Napoleon-like treats (*Kager*) layered with preserves and whipped cream.

---

1 teaspoon vinegar

¾ cup ice-cold water

1¼ pounds (5 sticks) cold unsalted
    butter

4 cups all-purpose flour

Advance Preparation: Mix the vinegar with the water and refrigerate until needed.

1. Using a pastry knife, cut half the butter into the flour. The mixture should resemble coarse meal.

2. Add the chilled water mixture and form into a dough, with as little handling as possible. Allow the dough to rest, covered with plastic film, for ½ hour.

3. Knead the remaining half of the butter until it is soft and pliable and can be spread with a spatula.

4. Roll out the dough to a square ½-inch thick. Spread the softened butter over the dough and fold in half. Wrap in plastic film and allow to rest for ½ hour.

5. Roll the dough out again and fold in half. Repeat this until no butter flecks are seen in the dough. This should take 2 or 3 additional rolling and folding steps. Wrap in plastic film and refrigerate until needed. Use as described above or in the Notes.

Notes: To make pretzel pastries with this dough roll out the dough to ½-inch thickness and cut into 4-inch x 1½-inch strips. Bend each strip into a pretzel shape and brush with egg wash. Generously sprinkle with sugar and bake at 400 degrees F until golden brown, about 8 minutes.

Butter Horns

Smørhorn

Butter horns are similar to croissants in their method of preparation and shape. The dough encases butter and is repeatedly folded and rolled out, creating many layers of flaky, buttery pastry.

¾ cup milk, scalded and cooled to lukewarm

1 tablespoon dry yeast

1 tablespoon plus ¼ cup sugar

3 cups all-purpose flour

½ pound (2 sticks) unsalted butter

1 egg white

½ cup ground almonds

Advance Preparation: All advance preparation may be found in the ingredient list.

1. Sprinkle the yeast across the surface of the scalded warm milk. Allow the yeast to dissolve for 3 minutes. Stir to form a creamy mixture.

2. Mix 1 tablespoon of sugar with the flour and cut in 8 tablespoons of the butter, as for pie dough. The mixture should resemble coarse meal. Stir in the yeast mixture to form a smooth dough. Cover with a cloth and allow to rise until doubled in bulk, about 1 hour.

3. Roll the dough to ¼-inch thickness. Spread the remaining 8 tablespoons of butter across the surface. Fold the dough in thirds, as for a letter, and roll out again. Repeat until no flecks of butter can be seen in the dough. Wrap in plastic film and refrigerate 1 hour.

4. Roll the dough to ¼-inch thickness and cut into 3-inch squares. Cut each square diagonally into triangles. Roll up each triangle, starting at the wide base, ending at the point, pressing to seal the point to the roll. Place pastries on a parchment-lined baking sheet.

5. Beat the egg whites with 2 tablespoons water and brush each butter horn with this wash. Toss the ¼ cup sugar with the ground almonds and sprinkle over the pastries. Cover the pastries with a cloth and allow to rise until doubled in bulk, about 1 hour. Meanwhile heat oven to 375 degrees F.

6. Bake the pastries until golden brown, about 15 minutes.

Notes: For additional flavor add ½ teaspoon cinnamon or ground cardamom to the almond topping. For a more croissant-like roll, skip the almond topping.

Quick Coffee Bread

Makes 2 loaves

Gallop Kringle

This recipe skips the successive rollings and foldings of a proper kringle, but it is quite tasty and much easier to prepare. Rather than flaky, the dough is buttery and rich, much like a sweet brioche.

1¼ cups milk	1 teaspoon grated lemon zest
1 tablespoon dry yeast	about 5 cups all-purpose flour
½ cup sugar	½ cup chopped walnuts
12 tablespoons unsalted butter, at room temperature	½ cup raisins
2 eggs, beaten until frothy	1 teaspoon ground cardamom

Advance Preparation: Scald the milk over medium heat. Remove ¼ cup and allow it to cool to lukewarm. Keep the remaining milk hot.

1. Sprinkle the yeast over the ¼ cup scalded lukewarm milk. Allow the mixture to stand for 5 minutes.

2. Add the sugar and 8 tablespoons of the butter to the reserved 1 cup hot milk and stir to incorporate. Whisk in the beaten eggs and lemon zest. Allow mixture to cool to lukewarm.

3. Stir in the yeast mixture. Add the flour in portions to form a smooth, soft dough that does not stick to the hands. Knead for 5 minutes. Cover the dough with a damp cloth and allow to rise for 1½ hours in a warm, draft-free area.

4. Punch down the dough and divide in half. Roll each out to an oblong shape about ½-inch thick.

5. Spread the remaining 4 tablespoons of butter across the surface of the rolled out doughs. Toss together the walnuts, raisins, and cardamom. Distribute this mixture across the buttered surfaces.

6. Roll up each dough rectangle jelly-roll fashion and form into a pretzel shape. Place on a parchment-lined baking sheet, cover with a damp cloth and allow to rise until doubled in bulk, about 1 hour. Meanwhile heat the oven to 375 degrees F.

7. Bake the pastries until golden brown and well risen, about 30 minutes. Cool on wire racks.

Notes: For variety, pecans can replace the walnuts and cinnamon can replace the cardamom. Other dried fruit, such as plums or cherries can replace the raisins.

Danish Doughnuts

Æbleskiver

Preparation of these doughnuts requires a special pan (*æbleskivepande*) with seven wells to form round doughnuts. Batter is poured into each well and the doughnuts are traditionally turned with a long knitting needle, but a fork will do. These special pans can be ordered on-line and are called æbleskiver pans, Monk's pans, or Danish Doughnut pans.

---

3 eggs, separated

2 cups buttermilk

2 cups all-purpose flour

2 teaspoons baking powder

½ teaspoon baking soda

1 tablespoon sugar

pinch salt

oil or clarified unsalted butter for cooking

powdered or granulated sugar

Advance Preparation: Whip the egg whites to form stiff peaks that are not dry. If liquid separates upon standing, rebeat the egg whites before using.

1. Beat the egg yolks with the buttermilk.

2. Sift the flour with the baking powder, baking soda, sugar, and salt.

3. Stir the flour mixture into the buttermilk mixture to form a smooth batter. Gently fold in the beaten egg whites.

4. Heat the æbleskiver pan over high heat. Add 1 tablespoon of oil or butter to each well. Half fill each well with batter. When the batter bubbles and the sides begin to set, quickly flip them over to cook on the other side, using a long skewer or fork.

5. Rotate the doughnuts as they cook, to brown them evenly. The doughnuts are done when set in the centers and a skewer put in the center comes out clean.

6. While hot and right from the pan, toss the doughnuts in powdered or granulated sugar to coat. Serve immediately.

Notes: A dollop of jam or a wedge of apple may be inserted into the doughnuts before flipping. *Æbleskiver* translates to apple slices, and so placing an apple wedge in the center is quite traditional. A sliver of dried plum (prune) is also often inserted. Cardamom or lemon peel may be added to the batter and cinnamon can be added to granulated sugar to toss them in after cooking.

Cornets with Whipped Cream

Kræmmerhuse med Flødeskum

These popular treats are formed from baked circles of batter that are rolled into cone shapes while still hot, and will turn crisp as they cool.

2 cups heavy cream, chilled	3 tablespoons cold water
¾ cup sugar	1 cup all-purpose flour
3 eggs	

Advance Preparation: Whip the cream with 2 tablespoons of the sugar to form stiff peaks. Refrigerate until needed. Line baking sheets with parchment paper. Heat the oven to 400 degrees F.

1. Beat the remaining sugar with the eggs and water to form a light, pale mixture.

2. Stir in the flour to form a thick batter.

3. Spread spoonfuls of batter into thin 4-inch circles on the lined baking pans using a moistened spatula. Bake for about 5 minutes, or until the edges of the circles start to brown.

4. Remove the baked circles and quickly form them into cones while still hot. Use cone-shaped wine glasses to help hold the shape while cooling. The cones can be stacked as they cool to keep their shape until set.

5. Fill the cooled cones with the reserved whipped cream and serve at once.

Notes: A dollop of preserves can top each cone for added eye and taste appeal. Cooked and cooled fruit compote can replace the whipped cream. For a unique way to serve the cones, fill a deep bowl halfway with granulated sugar and set the filled cones upright into the sugar.

Apple Cake

Æblekage

This is not a baked cake; rather it is a layered treat much like a charlotte or trifle. It is very popular across Scandinavia, and many say that it is the most popular dessert in Denmark.

2 cups dry breadcrumbs, homemade from white or French bread, crushed fine with a rolling pin

4 tablespoons unsalted butter

3 tablespoons sugar

3 cups sweetened applesauce (see page 212)

sweetened whipped cream

Advance Preparation: Make the dry breadcrumbs (do not use prepared breadcrumbs from the market).

1. In a medium skillet, heat the butter over medium heat until it foams. Toss the breadcrumbs with the sugar and add them to the butter. Stir until the butter is absorbed and the breadcrumbs are crisp and golden brown, being careful not to burn the crumbs. Remove crumbs from the pan and allow to cool.

2. When cooled, place a thin layer of toasted breadcrumbs in the bottom of a glass serving bowl. Top with a thin layer of applesauce. Repeat the layering until all the applesauce and breadcrumbs are used, ending with a layer of breadcrumbs.

3. Top with sweetened whipped cream and serve at once. (If prepared too long in advance, the breadcrumbs will turn soggy.)

Notes: "Veiled Country Lass" (*Bondepige med Slør*) is a similar recipe, using dark rye breadcrumbs.

Danish Layer Cake

Dansk Lagkage

Danish cakes are most often baked in many thin layers, rather than the two or three thick layers usually found in American layer cakes. Fillings are usually fruit preserves and custard, with a topping of whipped cream.

½ pound (2 sticks) unsalted butter, softened	2 teaspoons baking powder
½ cup sugar	1 cup fruit preserves, such as raspberry, plum, or apricot
2 eggs	1 cup rich vanilla custard or pudding
½ cup milk	stiffly whipped cream, slightly sweetened
½ teaspoon vanilla extract	
2 cups all-purpose flour	

Advance Preparation: The custard can be made one day in advance. The whipped cream may be prepared several hours in advance (use 1 tablespoon sugar to 1 cup heavy cream). Heat the oven to 375 degrees F. Cut circles of parchment and place them into five 8-inch cake pans.

1. Beat the butter with the sugar until light and fluffy, about 3 minutes.

2. Whisk the eggs with the milk and vanilla.

3. Sift the flour twice with the baking powder.

4. Add the egg mixture in portions to the butter mixture, alternating with the flour mixture. Mix to form a smooth batter.

5. Divide the batter between the five cake pans (layers will be thin). Bake until brown, about 10 minutes. Remove cakes from pans and allow to cool on wire racks.

6. Spread preserves and custard on alternating layers of cake. Top the cake with whipped cream. The sides of the cake may be frosted with whipped cream if desired. Refrigerate several hours before serving.

Notes: The cake may be garnished with toasted chopped almonds. Almond extract can be added to the custard, but use sparingly, as almond extract is very strong.

Sour Cream Cake

Sur Fløde Kage

Sour cream is a common addition to Danish baked goods, providing additional moisture and richness to cake layers. The raisin filling is an interesting confection, cooked like candy to the soft-ball stage and then spread between layers and used as icing.

---

3 cups sugar

1 cup seedless raisins, chopped

pinch salt

2 eggs

1 cup rich sour cream (organic sour cream would be best)

1 tablespoon molasses

1½ cups all-purpose flour

1 teaspoon baking soda

1 teaspoon ground cinnamon

1 teaspoon grated nutmeg

⅛ teaspoon ground cloves

Advance Preparation: Heat 1 cup water to a boil. Stir in 2 cups of the sugar to dissolve. Add the chopped raisins and salt and cook over medium heat to the soft-ball stage. A candy thermometer should read 235 degrees F (or a portion of the filling may be dropped into a glass of cold water; when removed, the mixture should form a ball that can be flattened between fingers). Allow raisin mixture to cool and reserve until needed. Heat the oven to 350 degrees F. Cut circles of parchment and place them into four 8-inch cake pans.

1. Whisk the eggs until pale and fluffy. Beat in the remaining 1 cup sugar until dissolved. Stir in the sour cream and molasses.

2. Sift the flour with the baking soda and spices. Gently stir this mixture into the egg mixture to form a smooth batter.

3. Divide batter between the four cake pans and bake until golden brown, about 10 minutes. Remove cakes from pans and cool on wire racks.

4. Spread layers of cake with raisin filling, warming the filling if too stiff. Ice the top and sides with the filling also. Allow the cake to set for one hour before serving.

Notes: In some regions of Denmark, plum jam is used on alternate layers with raisin filling and whipped cream tops the cake.

Sand Cake

Sandkage

The texture of this cake is rather dry and grainy, hence the name. Do not be put off by this. Sand cake is delicious and stores well. A dusting of powdered sugar is all that this cake needs, along with a hot cup of strong coffee.

½ pound (2 sticks) unsalted butter, at room temperature

1 cup sugar

grated zest of 1 lemon

6 eggs, separated

2 tablespoons sherry or brandy

1 cup all-purpose flour

1 cup cornstarch

½ tablespoon baking powder

pinch salt

powdered sugar

Advance Preparation: Grease and flour a 9-inch tube pan. Heat the oven to 350 degrees F.

1. Beat the butter with the sugar until pale and fluffy. Stir in the lemon zest.

2. Beat in the egg yolks one at a time, beating well after each addition. Stir in the sherry or brandy.

3. Sift the flour with the cornstarch, baking powder, and salt. Stir into the butter mixture to form a smooth batter.

4. Whip the egg whites until stiff but not dry or cracking. Carefully fold them into the batter until uniform in texture.

5. Pour the batter into the prepared pan. Bake until done, about 45 minutes. Allow the cake to cool in the pan.

6. Remove the cake from the pan and dust with powdered sugar.

Notes: A confectionary glaze may be drizzled over the cake when cool. Mix powdered sugar with water or orange juice to form a thick, but pourable glaze.

Seven Sisters' Cake

Søsterkage

This is a very old recipe. A special cake pan with corrugated sides is used. Danish recipes for Seven Sisters' Cake date back to 1700. On Samsoe Island, off the coast of Jutland, this cake is baked for Christmas with the addition of candied fruits, such as citron and Seville orange. The Danes are historically linked to the sea, and navigation by the stars was the method by which they sailed. The cake is named after the star cluster Pleiades, also known in Greek mythology as the Seven Sisters of Pleiades.

---

1 cup milk

1 tablespoon dry yeast

3 cups all-purpose flour

½ pound (2 sticks) unsalted butter, at room temperature

3 eggs

1 teaspoon ground cardamom

½ cup raisins

heavy cream

sugar

Advance Preparation: Scald the milk. Allow it to cool to lukewarm.

1. Sprinkle the yeast over ¼ cup of lukewarm scalded milk. Allow the mixture to stand 2 minutes. Stir to combine.

2. Stir 1 cup of flour into the remaining milk to form a smooth paste. Stir in the yeast mixture and allow this to stand for 1 hour in a warm, draft-free area.

3. Heat the oven to 350 degrees F. Beat the butter until pale in color. Add the eggs one at a time, beating well after each addition. Beat 1 minute. Stir in the yeast mixture and cardamom.

4. Add the remaining 2 cups flour and stir to form a smooth, thick batter that can be poured. Fold in the raisins and pour the batter into an ungreased 9-inch loaf pan.

5. Brush the top with cream and sprinkle generously with sugar. Bake for about 45 minutes, or until set in the center. Allow the cake to cool in the pan on a wire rack.

Notes: For Christmas bread add ½ cup diced candied citron and ½ cup candied orange peel. A heavy dusting of powdered sugar after baking can replace the glaze applied before baking.

Butter Cake

Serves 8

Smørkage

No one does butter better than the Danes and this cake celebrates the outstanding quality of this important dairy product. In addition to buttery yeast dough, the cake is filled with a butter filling and rich custard to which butter has been added.

Custard:
2 eggs
¼ cup sugar
½ cup all-purpose flour
2 cups half and half or light cream
1 teaspoon vanilla extract
2 tablespoons unsalted butter

Butter Filling:
8 tablespoons unsalted butter, at
    room temperature
¼ cup powdered sugar
¼ cup currants

Dough:
1½ cups all-purpose flour
8 tablespoons unsalted butter
1 tablespoon dry yeast
½ cup sugar
1 egg

Advance Preparation: The custard and butter filling should be made several hours in advance to allow the custard to cool and the filling to set. Grease a 9-inch springform pan.

1. To make the custard, beat the eggs with the sugar until light and fluffy. Stir in the flour to form a smooth mixture. Scald the cream and add the vanilla. Whisk this into the flour mixture and return to the pan. Cook over low heat and allow the custard to simmer, without boiling, for 2 minutes. Whisk in the butter and allow the custard to cool.

2. To make the butter filling, beat the butter with the powdered sugar and stir in the currants.

3. To make the dough, sift the flour and cut in the butter with a pastry knife. Dissolve the yeast into ¼ cup warm water along with the sugar. Whisk the egg into the yeast mixture and stir this into the flour mixture to form a smooth dough. Allow the dough to rise, covered, in a warm, draft-free area until doubled in bulk, about 1½ hours.

4. Turn the dough onto a floured surface and knead for 5 minutes, adding additional flour as necessary. Roll ⅓ of the dough into a 9-inch circle. Place it into the prepared springform pan. Spread the custard over the dough.

5. Roll the remaining dough into a rectangle about 4-inches wide. Spread the butter filling across the surface, leaving a ½-inch border without filling. Roll the dough up jelly-roll fashion starting on the long side and slice into 9 spiral rounds.

6. Place these rounds on top of the custard in the pan. Cover the cake with a cloth and allow to rise 1 hour in a warm, draft-free area. Meanwhile heat the oven to 375 degrees F.

7. Bake for 30 minutes or until golden and set in the center. Allow to cool in the pan on a wire rack.

Notes: When cool, the cake may be decorated with rosettes of buttercream frosting flavored with rum.

Othello Cake

Othello Lagkage

Fanciful names are often given to Danish desserts and pastries. Othello cake has a surprise concealed inside—a crunchy almond meringue layer nestled between layers of sponge cake.

Custard filling:

2 eggs

¼ cup sugar

½ cup all-purpose flour

2 cups half and half or light cream

1 teaspoon vanilla extract

2 tablespoons unsalted butter

Meringue:

⅔ cup finely ground almonds or
    almond flour if available

¼ cup sugar

1 teaspoon baking powder

2 egg whites, at room temperature

Sponge Cake:

3 eggs

½ cup sugar

½ cup all-purpose flour

½ cup potato starch

1 teaspoon baking powder

8 ounces almond paste or marzipan

Advance Preparation: The meringue layer can be made one day in advance, wrapped in plastic film and stored in a dry, room temperature place. Line the bottoms of three 9-inch cake pans with parchment paper. Heat the oven to 325 degrees F.

1. To make the custard, beat the eggs with the sugar until light and fluffy. Stir in the flour to form a smooth mixture. Scald the cream and add the vanilla. Whisk this into the flour mixture and return to the pan. Cook over low heat and allow the custard to simmer, without boiling, for 2 minutes. Whisk in the butter and allow the custard to cool.

2. To make the meringue, toss the ground almonds with the sugar and baking powder. Whip the egg whites stiff, but not dry or cracking. Gently fold the almond mixture into the egg whites to form a smooth batter. Pour the batter into one of the prepared pans and bake at 325 degrees F for 20 minutes or until golden and crisp. Store the meringue wrapped in plastic film until needed.

3. To make the sponge cake layers, beat the eggs with the sugar until pale and thick. Sift the flour with the potato starch and baking powder. Stir this into the egg mixture to form a smooth batter.

4. Pour cake batter into the remaining two prepared pans and bake for about 10 minutes or until set in the centers. Allow to cool in the pans on wire racks.

5. To assemble the cake, spread half of the custard onto a sponge cake layer. Add the meringue layer and spread the remaining custard over. Top with the second sponge cake layer.

6. Roll out the almond paste between sheets of plastic film to a circle twice the diameter of the cake. Gently drape the cake in the almond paste. With hands dusted in powdered sugar, form the almond paste snugly around the cake, trimming any excess at the base with a sharp paring knife.

7. Refrigerate the cake for 1 hour before slicing.

Notes: The almond paste can be replaced by whipped cream or chocolate icing, or a combination of the two.

Sour Cream Coffee Cake

Sur Fløde Kaffeekage

This recipe can be assembled and baked on the spur of the moment, providing a wonderful accompaniment to a casual cup of coffee with friends.

½ pound (2 sticks) unsalted butter, at room temperature

¾ cup sugar

2 eggs

⅓ cup sour cream

1¼ cups all-purpose flour

1 teaspoon baking powder

½ teaspoon baking soda

pinch salt

½ cup crushed cornflakes

½ cup brown sugar

Advance Preparation: Grease an 8-inch square pan. Heat the oven to 375 degrees F.

1. Beat the butter with the sugar until light and fluffy. Beat in the eggs, one at a time, beating well after each addition. Stir in the sour cream.

2. Sift the flour with the baking powder, baking soda, and salt. Gently stir this into the butter mixture, forming a smooth batter.

3. Pour the batter into the prepared pan. Mix the crushed cornflakes with the brown sugar and crumble this mixture over the surface of the cake.

4. Bake for 20 minutes or until golden and set in the center. Cool in the pan on a wire rack.

Notes: A more traditional streusel topping may replace the cornflake mixture. Mix ¼ cup flour with ¼ cup brown sugar. Cut in 4 tablespoons butter. Add a pinch of cinnamon and roll the mixture between your palms to form small lumps.

Tosca Torte

Toscatærte

Danish cakes are often multi-layered confections with rich fillings. This torte is baked in a tart pan as a single layer, with a decadent caramelized almond topping to finish.

Cake:
2 eggs
⅔ cup sugar
2 tablespoons dark brown sugar
4 tablespoons unsalted butter, melted
grated zest of 1 orange
1⅓ cups all-purpose flour
½ tablespoon baking powder
¼ cup heavy cream

Topping:
4 tablespoons unsalted butter
¼ cup sugar
¾ cup skinless almonds, coarsely chopped
2 tablespoons heavy cream
2 tablespoons all-purpose flour

Advance Preparation: Grease a 9-inch tart pan with a removable bottom. Heat the oven to 350 degrees F.

1. To make the cake, beat the eggs with the sugar until pale and thick. Stir in the melted butter and orange zest. Sift the flour with the baking powder and stir this into the egg mixture, forming a smooth batter. Stir in the cream.

2. Spread the batter into the prepared pan. Bake at 350 degrees F for 20 minutes. Increase the heat to 400 degrees F and continue baking while the topping is prepared, about 10 minutes.

3. Place the topping ingredients in a heavy saucepan. Heat the mixture to a boil, stirring occasionally.

4. Spread this topping over the cake and continue to bake at 400 degrees F for 15 minutes or until the cake is golden brown. Allow the cake to cool in the pan on a wire rack.

Notes: If bitter almonds are available, grate 3 to replace the orange zest.

Cardamom Cake

Kardemommenkage

Cardamom is a familiar spice to Scandinavian bakers. It was introduced from Constantinople by the Vikings around 1000 AD. Today it is one of the most-often-used spices in Danish baking. This cake celebrates the citrus perfume of this ginger-related plant.

½ pound (2 sticks) unsalted butter, at room temperature

1 cup sugar

3 eggs

3½ cups all-purpose flour

1 tablespoon baking powder

1 teaspoon ground cardamom (see Notes)

⅔ cup milk

¼ cup raisins

1 tablespoon grated lemon zest

1 tablespoon grated orange zest

¼ cup finely chopped skinless almonds

Advance Preparation: Grease a 9-inch loaf pan. Heat the oven to 375 degrees F.

1. Beat the butter with the sugar until light and fluffy, about 3 minutes. Beat in the eggs, one at a time, beating well after each addition.

2. Sift the flour with the baking powder and cardamom. Stir this into the butter mixture, alternating with portions of the milk, forming a smooth batter.

3. Stir in the raisins, lemon and orange zest, and almonds.

4. Pour the batter into prepared pan and bake for about 1 hour, or until the cake is set in the center and golden brown. Cool in the pan on a wire rack.

Notes: As with all spices, grinding fresh releases the most aroma and flavor. Use about 10 green cardamom pods and crush them with a mortar and pestle.

Almond Cake

Mandelkage

Almonds make their way into so many cuisines of the world. They are particularly desirable in desserts as they add richness and flavor, especially when toasted or roasted. Ground almonds are added to many European tortes, and almonds are processed into marzipan and almond paste. This paste can be rolled out and draped over a cake or molded into fanciful fruit shapes and then made realistic with vegetable dyes.

½ cup sugar

1½ cups all-purpose flour

1 teaspoon baking powder

8 tablespoons unsalted butter

2 eggs

¾ cup coarsely ground almonds (see Notes)

⅔ cup powdered sugar

Advance Preparation: Heat the oven to 375 degrees F.

1. Mix the sugar with the flour and baking powder. Cut in the butter with a pastry knife or pulse the mixture using a food processor to form coarse meal.

2. Beat 1 of the eggs and blend it into the butter mixture, forming a firm dough. Divide the dough in half.

3. Mix the ground almonds with the powdered sugar. Beat in the remaining egg.

4. Spread half of the dough into an 8-inch tart pan with removable bottom. Spread the almond mixture over the dough.

5. Divide the remaining dough into portions to roll into ½-inch ropes. Place these crisscross, in a lattice pattern, over the almond mixture. If any dough is left, use it to circle the edge of the pan.

6. Bake for 30 minutes or until golden and set. Allow the cake to cool on a wire rack before serving in wedges.

Notes: To grind almonds in a food processor, add some sugar or powdered sugar to the almonds to prevent them from forming almond paste.

Sour Cream Chocolate Cake

Chokoladekiksekage

Some of the world's best chocolate is produced in nearby European countries. Combined with Danish butter and sour cream, you have an irresistible dessert for kids of all ages!

Cake:

8 tablespoons unsalted butter, at room temperature

1 cup sugar

2 egg yolks (the whites are used in the frosting)

1 teaspoon baking soda

½ cup sour cream

1 teaspoon vanilla extract

1½ cups all-purpose flour

1 teaspoon baking powder

¼ cup cocoa powder

¼ cup hot water

3 ounces bittersweet or dark chocolate, melted

Filling:

2 tablespoons cornstarch

1 tablespoon cocoa powder

⅔ cup sugar

1 tablespoon unsalted butter, melted

1 teaspoon vanilla extract

Frosting:

½ cup sugar

⅓ cup brown sugar

¼ cup hot water

2 egg whites, beaten stiff but not dry

Advance Preparation: Grease and flour two 9-inch round cake pans. Heat the oven to 350 degrees F. The frosting and filling may be made in advance.

1. To make the cake, beat the butter with the sugar until light and fluffy. Beat in the egg yolks.

2. Stir the baking soda into the sour cream to dissolve. Whisk this into the butter mixture. Add the vanilla.

3. Sift the flour with the baking powder and stir this into the butter mixture.

4. Mix the cocoa with the ¼ cup hot water to form a smooth paste. Stir this into the batter.

5. Whisk the melted chocolate into the batter and pour into the prepared pans.

6. Bake for 20 minutes or until set in the center. Allow the cakes to cool in the pans on a wire rack while preparing the filling and frosting.

7. For the filling, sift the cocoa with the cornstarch. Mix in the sugar. Put this in a heavy saucepan and stir in 1 cup of water. Add the melted butter and whisk in the vanilla. Cook over low heat for 10 minutes, stirring occasionally. Allow the custard to cool before filling the cake.

8. For the frosting, mix the sugar and brown sugar with ¼ cup hot water. Boil in a heavy saucepan until the mixture forms threads when pulled from the surface, about 230 degrees F on a candy thermometer. Whisk the hot syrup into the beaten egg whites to form a smooth frosting. Allow to cool before frosting the cake.

9. Top one of the cooled cake layers with the cooled filling. Add the second layer and cover the cake with the frosting. Refrigerate several hours before serving.

Notes: Melted chocolate beaten with a little butter can be drizzled over the frosted cake as decoration.

Poppy Seed Cake

Valmuefrøkage

Poppy seeds have been used for centuries throughout Europe in pastry and desserts. The seeds are from the opium poppy and do contain small amounts of alkaloids. The filling for this decadent dessert is a rich hazelnut custard, and hazelnuts garnish the frosting as well.

Cake:

½ cup poppy seeds (see Notes)

1 cup warm milk

1 teaspoon vanilla extract

12 tablespoons unsalted butter, at room temperature

1½ cups sugar

2 cups all-purpose flour

½ tablespoon baking powder

4 egg whites (the yolks will be used in the filling)

Filling:

4 egg yolks

¾ cup sugar

2 tablespoons cornstarch

1½ cups milk

½ teaspoon vanilla extract

¾ cup finely chopped roasted hazelnuts (see Notes)

Frosting:

1 cup powdered sugar

2 tablespoons dark rum

¾ cup finely chopped roasted hazelnuts

Advance Preparation: Soak the poppy seeds in the milk mixed with the vanilla overnight. Grease and flour two 8-inch round cake pans. Heat the oven to 350 degrees F.

1. For the cake, beat the butter with the sugar until light. Sift the flour with the baking powder and stir it into the butter mixture in portions, alternating with the poppy seeds and soaking liquid. Whip the egg whites stiff but not dry and gently fold them into the batter.

2. Pour the batter into the prepared pans and bake for 20 minutes or until the cakes are set in the center. Allow the cakes to cool in the pans on a wire rack before removing from the pans, and then carefully cut each in half horizontally, forming 4 thin cake layers.

3. For the filling, whisk the egg yolks with the sugar until pale. Beat in the cornstarch and stir this mixture with the milk in a heavy saucepan. Add the vanilla and cook over low heat, until thick and just simmering. Cook an additional minute over very low heat, stirring constantly. Stir in the hazelnuts and allow the filling to cool before using.

4. Assemble cake by spreading the filling on the cake layers, stacking them as you go.

5. For the frosting, combine the powdered sugar with the rum to form a smooth mixture. Adjust the consistency for spreading with water, one tablespoon at a time, if necessary.

6. Frost the filled cake with the frosting. Garnish the frosting with roasted hazelnuts.

Notes: Poppy seeds contain oils that become rancid quickly. Be sure to use fresh poppy seeds. To skin and roast hazelnuts, place them on a baking pan in one layer and roast at 350 degrees F until the skins are dark and just starting to smoke. When cool, rub them in your hands or in a kitchen towel and the skins will fall right off. The hazelnuts can then be chopped in a food processor.

Applesauce Cake

Æblesaucekage

Apples are the quintessential cold climate fruit. The trees require a winter chill and the fall fruits last in cold storage over the long winters and well into summer.

---

8 tablespoons unsalted butter, at room temperature

2 cups sugar

1 egg

1½ cups unsweetened applesauce (see recipe page 212, omitting the sugar)

2½ cups all-purpose flour

1 teaspoon ground cinnamon

1 teaspoon ground allspice

¼ teaspoon ground cloves

1 teaspoon baking powder

2 teaspoons baking soda

¾ cup toasted chopped almonds (see Notes)

1 cup raisins

½ cup buttermilk

powdered sugar

Advance Preparation: If using homemade applesauce, it will need to be prepared in advance. Grease and flour a 10-inch square pan. Heat the oven to 350 degrees F.

1. Beat the butter with the sugar until light. Whisk in the egg and applesauce.

2. Sift the flour with the cinnamon, allspice, cloves, baking powder, and baking soda.

3. Mix the almonds and raisins together with a few tablespoons of the flour mixture.

4. Stir the flour mixture into the butter mixture, alternating with the buttermilk, to form a smooth batter. Fold in the almond mixture.

5. Put batter in prepared pan and bake for about 1 hour, or until the cake is golden and set in the center. Cool on a wire rack.

6. To serve, dust the applesauce cake with powdered sugar and cut into squares.

Notes: To toast almonds, heat a dry, heavy skillet over medium-low heat. Add the almonds and stir constantly. Lower the heat as the almonds become fragrant. When they just start to brown, remove them from the hot pan to cool.

Whipped Cream Cake

Flødekage

This is a very unusual recipe, one that only the Danes could create. Who else would use whipped cream as the base to fold in flour to make a cake batter?

1 cup heavy cream, well chilled	1½ cups all-purpose flour
1 cup sugar	½ tablespoon baking powder
2 eggs	1 teaspoon vanilla extract

Advance Preparation: Heat the oven to 350 degrees F.

1. Whip the cream to form stiff peaks, adding the sugar halfway through the whipping process.

2. Whisk in the eggs, one at a time.

3. Sift the flour with the baking powder and gently fold this into the whipped cream mixture. Stir in the vanilla.

4. Pour the batter into an ungreased 9-inch loaf pan and bake for 20 minutes or until set in the center.

5. Allow the cake to cool thoroughly in the pan before serving.

Notes: The bowl and whisk used to whip the cream should be cold and the cream thoroughly chilled.

Gingerbread

Ingefærkage

Gingerbread's origins are in Europe. It first appears as a digestive aid in the 12th century. But the gingerbread was quite hard. As the spice became more accessible and cheaper to buy, its popularity spread to baking and gingerbread in its modern form can be found in most European countries and across America.

½ pound (2 sticks) unsalted butter, at room temperature
1 cup sugar
1 cup molasses
2 teaspoons baking soda
1 cup buttermilk
2½ cups all-purpose flour

½ tablespoon ground ginger
1 teaspoon ground cinnamon
1 teaspoon ground allspice
4 eggs
freshly whipped cream

Advance Preparation: Grease and flour two 9-inch loaf pans. Heat the oven to 325 degrees F.

1. Beat the butter with the sugar until light and airy. Whisk in the molasses.

2. Mix the baking soda with the buttermilk and allow this to stand 2 minutes to become bubbly.

3. Sift the flour with the ginger, cinnamon, and allspice. Add to the butter mixture, alternating with the buttermilk mixture. Stir to form a smooth batter.

4. Whisk the eggs into the batter, one at a time. Pour the batter into the prepared pans.

5. Bake for about 1 hour, or until each loaf is set in the center. Cool in the pans on wire racks. Serve warm, topped with whipped cream.

Notes: For a tasty addition, plump ½ cup raisins in warm orange juice and stir them into the batter. Chopped hazelnuts or pecans can replace ½ cup of flour.

Marzipan Cakes

Kransekager

The origin of marzipan is not clear, but Persia and Spain are cited most often. Whether molded into fanciful shapes, rolled to enrobe a cake, or baked into delicate treats, marzipan is very rich and a little goes a long way. These cakes can be baked as concentric circles and then stacked to resemble a Christmas tree, or cut into logs to be eaten as little cakes.

---

1 pound (about 3 cups) ground almonds or almond flour

1 cup powdered sugar

½ cup sugar

3 egg whites

Icing:

1¼ cups powdered sugar

1 egg white

½ teaspoon white vinegar

Advance Preparation: Line baking sheets with parchment paper. Heat the oven to 300 degrees F.

1. Mix the almonds with the powdered sugar and sugar. Stir in 2 tablespoons water and the egg whites.

2. Place mixture in a heavy saucepan and cook over low heat, stirring often, until the almonds are slightly roasted and aromatic. Allow the mixture to cool thoroughly.

3. Form the dough into ½-inch-thick logs. Cut them into 2-inch lengths and place on the prepared baking sheets. Bake until the tops of the cakes are just browned. Cool on wire racks.

4. To make the icing, stir the powdered sugar with the egg white and vinegar until smooth.

5. When the cakes are cool drizzle icing over in a zigzag pattern.

Notes: To make a clever Christmas treat, bake the marzipan as round cookies, each one a bit smaller than the last. Drizzle each with icing when cooled and stack them to form a conical tree. Drizzle with more icing and use candied fruit as lights. A candied cherry on top finishes.

Jewish Cakes

Makes 2 dozen

Jødekager

The origin of this recipe is unknown as is its name. Jewish presence in Denmark began in 1622 when Jews were invited to live in Gliickstadt. By 1693 the first Jewish cemetery was established in Copenhagen.

---

6 tablespoons unsalted butter, at room temperature

⅓ cup sugar, reserving 1 tablespoon for topping

1 egg, separated

grated zest of 1 lemon

1 cup all-purpose flour

½ teaspoon baking soda

pinch salt

1-inch piece vanilla bean, optional

¼ cup chopped toasted almonds (see Notes)

Advance Preparation: The dough will need to be chilled for several hours before baking. Line baking sheets with parchment paper.

1. Beat the butter with the sugar. Beat in the egg yolk to form a smooth mixture. Stir in the lemon zest.

2. Sift the flour with the baking soda and salt. Mix this into the butter mixture to form a smooth dough. Divide and shape the dough into two logs approximately 2 inches in diameter. Chill thoroughly.

3. Heat the oven to 350 degrees F. Cut ¼-inch-thick slices of chilled dough and arrange them on prepared baking sheets close together to avoid spreading.

4. If using the vanilla bean, pound it with the reserved 1 tablespoon sugar in a mortar with a pestle or pulse in a food processor. Add the almonds and stir to form the topping.

5. Brush each cookie with egg white and sprinkle almond topping over each. Bake for 10 minutes or until golden brown and crisp. Cool on wire racks.

Notes: To toast nuts, warm a heavy skillet over medium heat. Add the nuts in one thin layer and lower the heat. Stir constantly until the nuts are aromatic and just beginning to brown. Shut off the heat and allow the pan to stay on the hot burner. Stir occasionally until cooled.

Danish Short Bread

Makes about 2 dozen cookies

Finsk Brød

To a baker the term "short" dough means high fat content dough that is crumbly in nature. When Danish bakers make a short dough, butter is always the fat used in high proportion.

⅔ cup sugar

10 ounces (2½ sticks) unsalted butter, at room temperature

1 egg

3 cups all-purpose flour

Advance Preparation: Line baking sheets with parchment paper. Heat the oven to 375 degrees F.

1. Beat the sugar with the butter until light and fluffy. Whisk in the egg.

2. Stir in the flour to form a smooth, firm dough.

3. Roll out the dough to ½-inch thickness. Cut the dough into diamond shapes and place them on the baking sheets.

4. Bake for 8 to 10 minutes or until golden brown. Cool on wire racks.

Notes: A mixture of chopped almonds and sugar can be dusted over the cookies before baking. The dough may also be baked in 8-inch rounds and cut into wedges while still warm.

Denmark's involvement in World War II contains some unique aspects with regard to German occupation and persecution of Jews. Soon after conquering it with little resistance from this small country, Germany declared Denmark a "model protectorate," allowing freedoms not seen in other occupied countries. The Danes declared there was no "Jewish problem" and for a while Germany tolerated Denmark's position. This would not last long and eventually this relationship collapsed and the Nazis began an attempt to round up Jews for export to concentration camps. Surprisingly the Danes rallied and saved the lives of thousands of Jews by coordinating, at all levels of government and the underground, the transportation of Jews by boats of all sizes and uses across the Øresund Straight to Sweden. In addition to having the fewest casualties of Jews among occupied Europe, Denmark's returning Jews found their homes and possessions intact, waiting for their return.

Sour Cream Cookies

Sur Fløde Kager

Sour cream adds both richness and tenderness to these traditional Christmas cookies. They can be made into fanciful shapes with your favorite cookie cutters.

1½ cups sugar
½ pound (2 sticks) unsalted butter, at room temperature
2 eggs
1 cup sour cream, at room temperature

1 teaspoon baking soda
1 teaspoon vanilla extract
2½ cups all-purpose flour
sugar

Advance Preparation: Line baking sheets with parchment paper. Heat the oven to 375 degrees F.

1. Beat the sugar with the butter until pale and fluffy. Beat in the eggs, one at a time, beating well after each addition.

2. Stir in the sour cream, baking soda, and vanilla. Mix in the flour to form a smooth dough that can be rolled out, adding a bit more flour if the dough is too sticky.

3. Roll out the dough to ½-inch thickness and cut into shapes with cookie cutters. Place the cookies on the baking sheets and sprinkle with sugar.

4. Bake for 8 to 10 minutes or until golden brown. Cool on wire racks.

Notes: A pinch of cinnamon or cardamom added to the dough would be a tasty addition. For more holiday spirit use colored sugar on the cookies.

Almond Rings

Makes about
18 cookies

Mandel Kranse

The delicate texture of these cookies comes from incorporating potato flour into the recipe. Not to be confused with potato starch, potato flour is made from whole potatoes, skins and all, and imparts a flavor missing from potato starch.

½ pound (2 sticks) unsalted butter, at room temperature

1 cup sugar

2 eggs

1 tablespoon cream

2 cups all-purpose flour

1 cup potato flour (see Notes)

1 teaspoon baking soda

½ cup ground almonds

Advance Preparation: Line baking sheets with parchment paper. Heat the oven to 375 degrees F.

1. Beat the butter with the sugar until light and fluffy. Beat in the eggs, one at a time, beating well after each addition. Stir in the cream.

2. Sift the flours and baking soda together. Toss in the almonds.

3. Add the flour mixture to the butter mixture to form a smooth, firm dough.

4. Roll the dough into ½-inch-diameter ropes and cut into 3-inch lengths. Form each length into a circle and place on the lined cookie sheets. (A cookie press may be used to extrude lengths of dough to be cut into sections.)

5. Bake for 8 to 10 minutes or until golden brown and crisp. Cool on wire racks.

Notes: A reasonable substitute for potato flour would be ¼ cup all-purpose flour mixed with ¼ cup instant potato flakes. Pulse this mixture in a food processor until uniform. Do not use potato starch as a substitute for potato flour.

196   **Part 2** Baking Traditions

Brunkager

These cookies are delightfully crisp and scented with sweet spices. If you can find ammonium carbonate (hartshorn), substitute for the baking soda. It will make the cookies even crisper.

½ pound (2 sticks) unsalted butter, at room temperature

1 cup brown sugar

1 cup molasses

4½ cups all-purpose flour

1 teaspoon ground cardamom

½ teaspoon ground allspice

¼ teaspoon ground cloves

pinch salt

1 teaspoon baking soda

grated zest of 1 small orange

Advance Preparation: The dough needs to be refrigerated at least 1 day and preferably 2 to 3 days.

1. Beat the butter with the brown sugar until light and airy. Whisk in the molasses.

2. Sift the flour with the cardamom, allspice, cloves, salt, and baking soda.

3. Mix the dry ingredients into the butter mixture to form a smooth dough. Stir in the orange zest. Form the dough into a 2-inch-diameter log. Wrap in plastic film and refrigerate at least one day and up to three days.

4. Heat the oven to 375 degrees F. Slice the chilled dough into very thin rounds and place them on a parchment-lined cookie sheet. Bake for 5 to 6 minutes, or until crisp. Cool on wire racks.

Notes: Be careful when baking as these cookies burn easily. They can be stored for long periods in tightly covered jars.

Sugar Cookies

**Makes about
3 dozen cookies**

Sukker Smaakager

With only four ingredients in this recipe be sure to use the best butter available, as it is the featured flavor in these delightful crisp sugar cookies.

---

1 pound (4 sticks) unsalted butter, at room temperature

2½ cups sugar

3 eggs, beaten, reserving 2 tablespoons to brush the cookies

4 cups all-purpose flour

Advance Preparation: Line baking sheets with parchment paper. Heat the oven to 375 degrees F.

1. Beat the butter with the sugar until light and fluffy. Gradually whisk in the beaten eggs. Stir in the flour to form a smooth dough.

2. Roll out the dough to ¼-inch thickness and cut out shapes with a cookie cutter. Place them on the lined cookie sheets. Brush with the reserved beaten egg and bake for 6 to 8 minutes, or until golden brown around the edges and crisp. Cool on wire racks.

Notes: The juice of ½ lemon or the grated zest of a lemon would be a tasty addition to this recipe.

Peppernuts

Pebernødder

Peppernuts can be found on almost every Christmas table in Europe. Originally a Dutch recipe, *pepernoten* were baked for Sinterklaas on December 5, when children receive gifts from St. Nicholas. Most recipes, including the German *pfeffernüsse*, add cinnamon and other sweet spices, and only a few add ground black pepper. The Danish version surprisingly omits all sweet spices and uses ground white pepper.

12 ounces (3 sticks) unsalted butter, at room temperature

1½ cups sugar

1 egg

1 teaspoon vanilla extract

5 cups all-purpose flour

2 teaspoons freshly ground white pepper

1 teaspoon baking soda

Advance Preparation: Line baking sheets with parchment paper. Heat the oven to 325 degrees F.

1. Beat the butter with the sugar until light and fluffy. Beat in the egg and vanilla.

2. Sift the flour with the pepper and baking soda. Add this to the butter mixture to form a smooth dough.

3. Roll the dough into ½-inch-diameter ropes. Cut them into ½-inch pieces and place on the lined cookie sheets.

4. Bake cookies for 10 minutes or until golden brown. Cool on wire racks.

Notes: While delicious plain, these cookies may be dipped in colored sugar before baking or may be generously covered in powdered sugar after baking while still warm.

Anise Cookies

Aniskager

Anise is a very sweet spice from the Mediterranean with flavors reminiscent of licorice. Extracts of the seed or the ground seed itself flavors liqueurs and baked goods around the world. While similar in flavor, star anise is not used in this manner.

4 eggs	grated zest of 2 lemons
3½ cups powdered sugar	4 cups all-purpose flour
1 teaspoon ground anise, or ¼ teaspoon anise oil	1 teaspoon baking powder
	almond halves

Advance Preparation: The dough must chill for several hours before rolling. The rolled cookies need to be refrigerated overnight before baking for best results. Line baking sheets with parchment.

1. Beat the eggs until thick and pale. Stir the powdered sugar, in portions, into the beaten eggs. Blend thoroughly. Mix in the anise and lemon zest.

2. Sift the flour with the baking powder and mix this into the egg mixture to form a stiff dough, adding more flour if necessary. Refrigerate dough for several hours, until well chilled.

3. The dough can be rolled out and cut into traditional shapes with cutters. Or for an authentic version, a springerle rolling pin with intricate designs carved into the surface can be used.

4. Place the formed cookies on the lined baking sheets and refrigerate overnight, covered in plastic film.

5. Heat the oven to 350 degrees F. Press an almond half into each cookie and bake for 30 minutes or until lightly browned. Cool on wire racks.

Notes: When cooled, place the cookies in airtight containers and they will last months if you have the willpower.

Cardamom Cookies

Kardemommekager

Next to saffron, cardamom is the most expensive spice and is celebrated in Danish baking, including these rich, spicy cookies.

1 egg
8 tablespoons unsalted butter,
    melted and cooled to lukewarm
1 cup sugar
1 cup all-purpose flour

½ teaspoon baking soda
1 teaspoon crushed cardamom
    seeds or ground cardamom
1 teaspoon ground cinnamon

Advance Preparation: Line baking sheets with parchment paper. Heat the oven to 350 degrees F.

1. Whisk the egg into the melted butter. Stir in the sugar and whisk 1 minute.

2. Sift the flour with the baking soda, cardamom, and cinnamon. Mix into the butter mixture to form a smooth dough.

3. Form the dough into 1-inch balls and place them on the lined cookie sheets. Flatten each ball with the back of a spoon and bake for 8 to 10 minutes or until the edges begin to brown and the cookies are set in the centers. Cool on wire racks.

Notes: Freshly crushed cardamom from pods would bring the best flavor to this recipe. If using ground cardamom, as with all ground spices, check for freshness before using. Cardamom should have a powerful sweet citrus aroma.

Caraway Cookies

Makes about
12 cookies

Kommenkager

Caraway is most often associated with rye and pumpernickel breads. Caraway "seeds" are not really seeds, but are the dried fruits of a biennial plant resembling carrots. The flavor is most appreciated in central and northern Europe, where it is found in breads and baked goods, liqueurs, cabbage dishes, and cheeses.

½ pound (2 sticks) unsalted butter, at room temperature

1 cup sugar

2 eggs

½ teaspoon baking soda

3 tablespoons buttermilk

2 cups all-purpose flour

1 tablespoon caraway seeds

sugar

Advance Preparation: The dough should be refrigerated for several hours before rolling and cutting. Line cookie sheets with parchment paper.

1. Beat the butter with the sugar until light and fluffy. Beat in the eggs, one at a time, beating well after each addition.

2. Stir the baking soda into the buttermilk and whisk this into the butter mixture.

3. Sift the flour into the butter mixture and add the caraway seeds and stir to form a smooth dough. Wrap the dough in plastic film and refrigerate 3 hours or overnight.

4. Heat the oven to 350 degrees F. Roll the dough to a thickness of ½-inch. Cut into fanciful shapes with cookie cutters, or with a sharp knife into diamonds, rectangles, etc. Place the cookies on the parchment-lined cookie sheets.

5. Sprinkle the cookies with sugar and bake for 20 minutes or until golden brown. Cool on wire racks.

Notes: These cookies may be glazed with an egg wash prior to, or instead of, the sugar topping. Beat one egg yolk with 2 tablespoons cream until uniform. Use a pastry brush to apply.

202   **Part 2** Baking Traditions

Copenhagen Cookies

Københavnerkager

When we think of Danish food in America, tins of Danish butter cookies quickly come to mind. These buttery and crisp delights are served on the Danish Christmas table with candied green and red cherries as garnish.

---

12 ounces (3 sticks) unsalted butter, at room temperature
½ cup sugar
2 cups all-purpose flour

1 egg, beaten
½ cup ground almonds

Advance Preparation: Line baking sheets with parchment paper. Heat the oven to 400 degrees F.

1. Beat the butter with the sugar and 1 tablespoon water until pale, about 3 minutes.

2. Sift the flour into the butter mixture and stir to form a smooth dough.

3. Roll the dough out thin on a floured surface and cut into shapes as desired. Place the cookies on the lined baking sheets. Brush the cookies with beaten egg and sprinkle with ground almonds.

4. Bake for 10 minutes or until the edges are brown and the cookies crisp. Cool on wire racks.

Notes: Candied fruits can be used to garnish the cookies for Christmas. Use halved candied cherries or citron cut into pleasing shapes.

Hazelnut Cookies

Hasselnødkager

These delicate cookies are made without flour and will spread quite a bit during baking. Roast and grind the fresh hazelnuts, also called filberts, for best results.

2½ cups hazelnuts or filberts

3 eggs

½ cup sugar

2 tablespoons hazelnut liqueur or brandy

2 tablespoons dry unseasoned breadcrumbs

Advance Preparation: Roast the hazelnuts in single layers on baking sheets at 325 degrees F until the papery skins are brown and just beginning to smoke, about 10 minutes. Remove the nuts from the oven and allow to cool in the pan. Rub the nuts between your hands and the skins will fall off. Discard the skins. Using a fine grating attachment to a food processor or mixer, grind the hazelnuts. Lower the oven to 300 degrees F.

1. Beat the eggs with the sugar and liqueur until pale and light, about 3 minutes. Mix in the ground hazelnuts and breadcrumbs.

2. Form the dough into small balls with your hands and place them on parchment-lined baking sheets about 3 inches apart.

3. Bake the cookies at 300 degrees F for 20 minutes or until golden brown and aromatic. Cool on wire racks.

Notes: The cookies may be garnished with hazelnut halves pressed into the dough balls before baking or with a sprinkling of sugar.

Vanilla Rings

Vaniljekranse

Only real vanilla can be used for these cookies. A vanilla bean would have been pounded with sugar in original recipes. If pure vanilla powder is not available use pure vanilla extract which should not contain added vanillin.

12 tablespoons unsalted butter, at
    room temperature

½ cup sugar

1 egg

½ tablespoon pure vanilla extract, or
    1 teaspoon vanilla powder (see
    Notes)

2 cups all-purpose flour

¼ cup ground almonds

Advance Preparation: Line baking sheets with parchment paper. Heat the oven to 400 degrees F.

1. Beat the butter with the sugar until pale and light. Beat in the egg and vanilla.

2. Mix the flour with the almonds and stir into the butter mixture until it forms a smooth dough that is not sticky.

3. Roll the dough into ½-inch-diameter ropes and cut them into 4-inch segments. Form the segments into circles and place these rings on the lined baking sheets.

4. Bake for 8 minutes or until lightly browned. Cool on wire racks.

Notes: An alternative to powdered vanilla would be to grind half of a fresh, quality vanilla bean with the ½ cup sugar in a food processor until uniform. Use this sugar to beat with the butter.

Danish Toast

Arme Riddere

This recipe is the Danish version of "French Toast" and is considered an evening snack or dessert rather than a breakfast or brunch item. The translation of both the Danish and German names for this dish is "Poor Knights." It is called "Poor Knights of Windsor" in England. This name presumably comes from the use of stale leftover bread to feed hungry troops who could not afford freshly baked bread. It is an excellent way to use stale bread.

4 eggs	¼ teaspoon ground cardamom
½ cup cream	8 thick slices stale white bread
pinch salt	dry unseasoned breadcrumbs
¼ cup sugar	butter
¼ teaspoon ground cinnamon	preserves or jam

Advance Preparation: Whisk the eggs with the cream, salt, sugar, cinnamon, and cardamom. Place this mixture in a shallow bowl or pan and add the bread slices in one layer. Set aside for about 1 hour to allow the bread to soak up the egg mixture completely.

1. Carefully dredge the soaked bread slices in breadcrumbs.

2. Heat some butter in a heavy skillet until it foams. Add the soaked bread, in batches if necessary, and fry 2 minutes on each side, or until golden and crisp on the edges. If frying in batches, place the cooked bread slices on a warm plate and cover with a cloth.

3. Serve warm with an assortment of preserves, jellies, or jams.

Notes: A generous dusting of powdered sugar makes an attractive presentation.

Bondepige med Slør

No one seems to know how this tasty way to use stale rye bread got its name. The bread should be dark and very dry. It is then grated, fried in butter, and layered with applesauce. A topping of whipped cream and a dab of raspberry preserves completes the dish.

---

8 thick slices dark rye or pumpernickel bread, preferably very stale

6 tablespoons unsalted butter

2 tablespoons sugar

2 cups applesauce (see page 212)

2 cups heavy cream

2 tablespoons seedless raspberry preserves

Advance Preparation: Place the bread slices in a warm oven to dry thoroughly, about 1 hour. Grate the bread to fine breadcrumbs.

1. Heat the butter in a heavy skillet until it foams. Add the dry breadcrumbs and sauté over medium heat 2 minutes. Sprinkle with sugar and cook 1 minute. Allow this mixture to cool.

2. In individual glasses or a serving bowl, alternate layers of breadcrumbs and applesauce. Chill individual parfaits 30 minutes or 1 hour for a serving bowl.

3. Whip the cream to form stiff peaks. Top the parfait(s) with whipped cream and dabs of raspberry preserves. Serve chilled.

Notes: One layer of applesauce may be replaced with preserves or whipped cream. For a chocolaty version add ¼ cup grated chocolate to the fried breadcrumbs while still hot.

Rice Fritters

Risengrynsklatter

The Danish twist to rice fritters is to use rich rice pudding as the base rather than rice alone. This makes for luscious and quite rich morsels. If you do not have any leftover rice pudding, make a fresh batch and use a portion to make these delectable fritters.

3 cups prepared rice pudding (see page 211)

1 egg

⅓ cup currants

¼ cup ground almonds

½ teaspoon ground cinnamon

grated zest of 1 lemon

½ cup all-purpose flour

unsalted butter for frying

preserves or jam

Advance Preparation: The rice pudding may need to be prepared ahead if using freshly made.

1. Mix the rice pudding with the egg. Stir in the currants, ground almonds, cinnamon, and lemon zest. Add as much of the flour as required to make a batter that holds its shape when dropped from a spoon.

2. Heat some butter in a heavy skillet until it foams. Drop large spoonfuls of rice batter into the butter and cook 2 minutes on each side, or until golden brown (do not crowd the pan).

3. Serve fritters warm with preserves or jam.

Notes: Prepared rice pudding can be found in most supermarkets and will save time, but homemade is superior.

Thin Pancakes

Tynde Pandekager

These delicate rolled pancakes are a Scandinavian favorite and are filled with fruit preserves or cinnamon sugar. They are larger and more fragile than a crêpe, but are cooked in the same manner.

4 eggs, separated

2 tablespoons sugar

1¼ cups all-purpose flour

2 cups milk

2 tablespoons unsalted butter, melted

pinch salt

pinch ground cardamom

seedless raspberry or lingonberry preserves

cinnamon sugar

Advance Preparation: Beat the egg whites to soft peaks.

1. Beat the egg yolks with the sugar until pale. Add the flour in portions, alternating with the milk. Stir to form a smooth batter. Whisk in the melted butter, salt, and cardamom.

2. Fold in the beaten egg whites until mixture is uniform and light. The batter will be very thin.

3. Heat a 10-inch non-stick skillet over medium heat. Brush with butter and ladle just enough batter to thinly coat the bottom of the pan, about ⅓ cup. Roll the pan to distribute the batter in a thin film. Pour any excess back into the batter bowl.

4. Turn the pancakes when the edges begin to curl. Cook briefly and slide the pancake to a warm plate. Repeat until all the batter is used.

5. Spread preserves on half of the pancakes and roll them cigar fashion. Sprinkle cinnamon sugar over the remaining pancakes and roll as before. Place them all on a platter and serve at once.

Notes: A bowl of freshly whipped cream to accompany would add a Danish touch to serving these thin pancakes.

Red Fruit Pudding

Serves 8 to 12

Rødgrød med Fløde

Puddings are popular across Scandinavia and this is the most popular of those puddings. Those who know best say three fruits are required to make a proper Red Fruit Pudding—red currants, raspberries, and cherries—but the real secret is to use fresh fruit to make the juice.

2 cups mixed unsweetened red fruit juice, such as cherry, raspberry, plum, and/or red currant

2 cups sugar (less if the juices are sweetened)

¼ teaspoon salt

1 cinnamon stick

1 vanilla bean, split open

¾ cup cornstarch

Advance Preparation: If fresh juice is to be used, boil about 1 pound of mixed fruit with 3 cups water until the berries have released all of their juice. Strain the mixture, pressing on the berry pulp to extract all liquid.

1. Heat the berry juice in a non-reactive saucepan with the sugar, salt, cinnamon stick, and vanilla bean. Bring to a boil and simmer 5 minutes over low heat. Remove the pan from the heat, cover and allow the juice to steep for 5 minutes.

2. Remove the cinnamon stick and vanilla bean and measure 2 cups of juice. Heat the juice to a simmer.

3. Add some water to the cornstarch to make a thin slurry. Pour this into the cooking juice in a stream, whisking as you add the slurry. The pudding should thicken quickly. Let the pudding come to a boil and remove immediately from the heat.

4. Pour into individual serving bowls and sprinkle the tops with sugar to prevent a crust from forming. Allow to cool and thicken before serving.

Notes: As with all things Danish, a bowl of whipped cream passed around the table would complement the pudding nicely.

Christmas Rice Pudding

Julerisengrød

A whole almond is placed into the rice pudding before serving. According to Danish lore the person who gets the almond in their portion on Christmas will have luck and adventure. In Sweden it is said the receiver of the almond will marry by the next Christmas Eve.

6 cups whole milk	1 whole almond, optional
1 cup raw rice	cinnamon
1 cup sugar	sugar
½ teaspoon salt	cream

Advance Preparation: The rice pudding will take about 3 hours to cook and should then be cooled before serving.

1. Place the milk, rice, sugar, and salt in the top of a double boiler. Cook over simmering water that does not touch the bottom of the top pot for about 3 hours or until the rice is soft and thick, stirring occasionally and checking the water level as it cooks.

2. Allow the pudding to cool to lukewarm before serving.

3. To serve, sprinkle the top of the pudding with cinnamon and sugar. Serve with a pitcher of cream on the side. If using the almond, place it in the pudding before topping with cinnamon.

Notes: Half of a split vanilla bean may be added to the cooking pudding. Toasted chopped almonds can be added to the cinnamon and sugar topping, or can replace it.

Applesauce

Æblegrød

Applesauce is a refreshing summer dessert in Denmark. It is also a staple for baked goods and desserts such as "Veiled Country Lass" (page 207). Use tart apples for best results. As the sauce will be strained, there is no need to peel or core the apples, making this an easy recipe to make on the spur of the moment.

3 pounds tart apples	sugar to taste

Advance Preparation: There is no advance preparation for this dish.

1. Quarter the apples but do not peel or core them.

2. Place the apples in a non-reactive saucepan and barely cover with cold water. Heat to a boil and lower the heat and simmer, uncovered, until the apples are very tender and easily pierced with the point of a knife.

3. Press the cooked apples through a strainer or sieve, removing spent skins and cores. Discard the cooking liquid or save it for a fruit soup recipe.

4. Add sugar to taste to the applesauce and allow to cool. Refrigerate until needed.

Notes: To preserve color, 2 teaspoons lemon juice may be added while cooking. For additional flavor add ½ teaspoon cinnamon to the strained applesauce. For recipes calling for unsweetened applesauce, leave out the sugar and do not add lemon juice.

Danish/English Culinary Terms

Aal; Ål Eel
Abrigos Apricot
Æble Apple
Æblegrød Applesauce
Æblesauce Applesauce
Æg Egg
Æggeblomme Egg yolk
Æggekage Omelet
Aerte Pea
Agerhøne Partridge
Agurke Cucumber
Ananas Pineapple
Anis Anise
Ansjos Anchovy
Appelsin Orange
Appetivækker Appetizer
Artiskok Artichoke
Asparges Asparagus
Aubergine Eggplant
Bacon Bacon
Bær Berry
Bage Bake
Bagværk Pastry
Banan Banana
Banke Stewed
Bede Beet
Beklagelse Beef
Biksemad Hash
Blæcksprutte Octopus
Blomkaal (Blomkål) Cauliflower
Bøf Steak
Boller Dumplings
Bolsje Candy
Bønne Bean
Brase Fry
Brød Bread; Loaf
Brombær Blackberry
Brun Brown, Browned
Brunede Caramelized
Byg Barley
Café Café
Cafeteria Cafeteria
Champignon Mushroom
Chokolade Chocolate

Citron Lemon
Dampskib Steamer
Dansk Danish
Delikatesse Delicatessen
Dessert Dessert
Dild Dill
Drukken Pickled
Duck Duck
Dybfrost Frozen Food
Dyrekød Venison
Får Mutton; Sheep
Farekød Mutton
Fasan Pheasant
Fedt Fat
Feinschmecker Gourmet
Fersken Peach
Figen Fig
Fisk Fish
Fjerkræ Poultry
Flæsk Pork
Flødeagtig Creamy
Flødeskum Whipped Cream
Frikadeller Meatballs
Frugt Fruit
Fryser Freezer
Fulde Pickled
Fyld Stuffing
Gås Goose
Gele Aspic
Gelé Jelly
Glaserede Glazed
Grapefrugt Grapefruit
Grav Cured
Grillere (v) Grill
Grøn Salat Lettuce
Grønstag Vegetable
Grøntsager Greens
Grynsklatter Fritters
Gylden Golden
Hakke (v) Chop
Hakke Mince
Hare Rabbit
Hasselnød Hazelnut
Helleflynder Halibut
Hindbær Raspberry

Hjemmelavet Homemade
Høne Chicken
Hummer Lobster
Hvede Wheat
Hvedemel Flour
Hvidkaal Cabbage
Hvidløg Garlic
Ingefær Ginger
Is Ice
Jordbær Strawberry
Jordnød Peanut
Kærnemælk Buttermilk
Kaffe Coffee
Kage Cake
Kager Cookies
Kalkun Turkey
Kål Cabbage
Kålsalat Coleslaw
Kanel Cinnamon
Kanin Rabbit
Karamel Caramel
Kardemom Cardamom
Karry Curry
Kartoffel Potato
Kasserole Saucepan
Kastanje Chestnut
Kedel Kettle
Kirsebær Cherry
Klejner Doughnuts
Kød Meat
Kødrand Meatloaf
Koge Boil
Kogebog Cookbook
Kogt Poached
Køkken Kitchen
Kokosnød Coconut
Kold Cold
Køleskab Refrigerator
Kommen Caraway
Korn Corn
Kørvel Chervil
Kotelet Chop (cut of meat)
Krabbe Crab
Kranse Ring
Krydderi Spice

Krydret Spicy	*Peberrod* Horseradish	*Solbær* Blackcurrant
Kylling Chicken	*Persil* Parsley	*Sovs* Gravy
Lakrids Licorice	*Pickles* Pickles	*Sovs* Sauce
Laks Salmon	*Pølse* Sausage	*Spinat* Spinach
Lam Lamb	*Pommes Frite* French Fries	*Spise* Eat
Lever Liver	*Postej* Pâté	*Spisekort* Menu
Likør Liqueur	*Purløg* Chives	*Sprød* Crisp
Løg Onion	*Rabarber* Rhubarb	*Steg* Roast; Fry
Madolie Salad oil	*Radise* Radish	*Stegeovn* Oven
Mælk Milk	*Reje* Prawn; Shrimp	*Stegepande* Frying Pan
Mager Lean	*Rensdyr* Reindeer	*Stegte* Flounder
Makrel Mackerel	*Ribben* Spare Ribs	*Stikkelsbær* Gooseberry
Mandarin Tangerine	*Ris* Rice	*Sukker* Sugar
Mandel Almond	*Riste* Roast	*Sulten* Hungry
Marinere Marinate	*Rivejern* Grater	*Suppe* Soup
Marineret Marinated	*Rørt* Creamed	*Suppelltalerken* Soup bowl
Marmelade Marmalade	*Rosenkål* Sprouts	*Sur* Sour
Mejeri Dairy	*Rug* Rye	*Sur fløde* Sour Cream
Melon Melon	*Saft* Juice	*Surkål* Sauerkraut
Middag Dinner	*Saftig* Juicy	*Svesker* Prunes
Mose Mash	*Salat* Salad	*Svin* Pig
Mosede Mashed	*Salt* Salt	*Svinekød* Pork
Muskat Nutmeg	*Saltkar* Saltshaker	*Sylte* Head Cheese
Musling Mussel	*Sardin* Sardine	*Tallerken* Plate
Mynte Mint	*Selleri* Celery	*Tilberde* Cook (*v*)
Nod Nut	*Sennep* Mustard	*Torsk* Cod
Oksekød Beef	*Sild* Herring	*Tunfisk* Tuna
Øl Beer	*Skål* Bowl	*Urt* Herb
Olie Oil	*Skaldyr* Shellfish	*Vaffel* Waffle
Oliven Olive	*Skinke* Ham	*Valmuefrø* Poppy Seed
Omelet Omelet	*Skorpe* Crust	*Valnød* Walnut
Ørred Trout	*Skorpor* Rusks	*Vand* Water
Ost Cheese	*Skræl* Peel *(n)*	*Vanille* Vanilla
Øster Oyster	*Skrælle* Peel *(v)*	*Varm* Warm
Ovn Stove	*Slagter* Butcher	*Vildt* Game
Pære Pear	*Smag* Flavor	*Vin* Wine
Pande Pan	*Småkage* Biscuit	*Vindruer* Grapes
Pandekager Pancakes	*Smelte* Melt	*Wienerbrød* Puff Pastry
Peber Pepper	*Smeltede* Melted	
Pebermynte Peppermint	*Smør* Butter	

English/Danish Culinary Terms

Almond *Mandel*
Anchovy *Ansjos*
Anise *Anis*
Appetizer *Appetivækker*
Apple *Æble*
Applesauce *Æblegrød, Æblesauce*
Apricot *Abrigos*
Artichoke *Artiskok*
Asparagus *Asparges*
Aspic *Gele*
Bacon *Bacon*
Bake *Bage*
Banana *Banan*
Barley *Byg*
Bean *Bønne*
Beef *Beklagelse; Oksekød*
Beer *Øl*
Beet *Bede*
Berry *Bær*
Biscuit *Småkage*
Blackberry *Brombær*
Blackcurrant *Solbær*
Boil *Koge*
Bowl *Skål*
Bread *Brød*
Brown/Browned *Brun*
Butcher *Slagter*
Butter *Smør*
Buttermilk *Kærnemælk*
Cabbage *Hvidkaal, Kål*
Café *Café*
Cafeteria *Cafeteria*
Cake *Kage*
Candy *Bolsje*
Caramel *Karamel*
Caramelized *Brunede*
Caraway *Kommen*
Cardamom *Kardemom*
Cauliflower *Blomkaal, Blomkål*
Celery *Selleri*
Cheese *Ost*
Cherry *Kirsebær*
Chervil *Kørvel*

Chestnut *Kastanje*
Chicken *Høne (Kylling)*
Chives *Purløg*
Chocolate *Chokolade*
Chop (cut of meat) *Kotelet;*
  (v) *Hakke*
Cinnamon *Kanel*
Coconut *Kokosnød*
Cod *Torsk*
Coffee *Kaffe*
Cold *Kold*
Coleslaw *Kålsalat*
Cook (v) *Tilberde*
Cookbook *Kogebog*
Cookies *Kager*
Corn *Korn*
Crab *Krabbe*
Creamed *Rørt*
Creamy *Flødeagtig*
Crisp *Sprød*
Crust *Skorpe*
Cucumber *Agurke*
Cured *Grav*
Curry *Karry*
Dairy *Mejeri*
Danish *Dansk*
Delicatessen *Delikatesse*
Dessert *Dessert*
Dill *Dild*
Dinner *Middag*
Doughnuts *Klejner*
Duck *Duck*
Dumplings *Boller*
Eat *Spise*
Eel *Aal; Ål*
Egg *Æg*
Egg white *Æggehvid*
Egg yolk *Æggeblomme*
Eggplant *Aubergine*
Fat *Fedt*
Fig *Figen*
Fish *Fisk*
Flavor *Smag*
Flounder *Stegte*
Flour *Hvedemel*

Freezer *Fryser*
French Fries *Pommes Frite*
Fritters *Grynsklatter*
Frozen Food *Dybfrost*
Fruit *Frugt*
Fry *Steg, Brase*
Frying Pan *Stegepande*
Game *Vildt*
Garlic *Hvidløg*
Ginger *Ingefær*
Glazed *Glaserede*
Golden *Gylden*
Goose *Gås*
Gooseberry *Stikkelsbær*
Gourmet *Feinschmecker*
Grapefruit *Grapefrugt*
Grapes *Vindruer*
Grater *Rivejern*
Gravy *Sovs*
Greens *Grøntsager*
Grill *Grillere (v)*
Halibut *Helleflynder*
Ham *Skinke*
Hash *Biksemad*
Hazelnut *Hasselnød*
Head Cheese *Sylte*
Herb *Urt*
Herring *Sild*
Homemade *Hjemmelavet*
Horseradish *Peberrod*
Hungry *Sulten*
Ice *Is*
Jelly *Gelé*
Juice/Juicy *Saft/Saftig*
Kettle *Kedel*
Kitchen *Køkken*
Lamb *Lam*
Lean *Mager*
Lemon *Citron*
Lettuce *Grøn Salat*
Licorice *Lakrids*
Liqueur *Likør*
Liver *Lever*
Loaf *Brød*
Lobster *Hummer*

Mackerel *Makrel*	Peanut *Jordnød*	Saucepan *Kasserole*
Marinate *Marinere*	Pear *Pære*	Sauerkraut *Surkål*
Marinated *Marineret*	Peel *Skrælle (v); Skræl (n)*	Sausage *Pølse*
Marmalade *Marmelade*	Pepper *Peber*	Sheep *Får*
Mash *Mose*	Peppermint *Pebermynte*	Shellfish *Skaldyr*
Mashed *Mosede*	Pheasant *Fasan*	Shrimp *Reje*
Meat *Kød*	Pickled *Fulde, Drukken*	Soup *Suppe*
Meatballs *Frikadeller*	Pickles *Pickles*	Soup bowl *Suppelltalerken*
Meatloaf *Kødrand*	Pig *Svin*	Sour *Sur*
Melon *Melon*	Pineapple *Ananas*	Sour Cream *Sur fløde*
Melt *Smelte*	Plate *Tallerken*	Spare Ribs *Ribben*
Melted *Smeltede*	Poached *Kogt*	Spice *Krydderi*
Menu *Spisekort*	Poppy Seed *Valmuefrø*	Spicy *Krydret*
Milk *Mælk*	Pork *Svinekød, Flæsk*	Spinach *Spinat*
Mince *Hakke*	Potato *Kartoffel*	Sprouts *Rosenkål*
Mint *Mynte*	Poultry *Fjerkræ*	Steak *Bøf*
Mushroom *Champignon*	Prawn *Reje*	Steamer *Dampskib*
Mussel *Musling*	Prunes *Svesker*	Stewed *Banke*
Mustard *Sennep*	Puff Pastry *Wienerbrød*	Stove *Ovn*
Mutton *Får, Farekød*	Quail *Vagtel*	Strawberry *Jordbær*
Nut *Nod*	Rabbit *Hare, Kanin*	Stuffing *Fyld*
Nutmeg *Muskat*	Radish *Radise*	Sugar *Sukker*
Octopus *Blæcksprutte*	Raspberry *Hindbær*	Tangerine *Mandarin*
Oil *Olie*	Refrigerator *Køleskab*	Trout *Ørred*
Olive *Oliven*	Reindeer *Rensdyr*	Tuna *Tunfisk*
Omelet *Æggekage, Omelet*	Rhubarb *Rabarber*	Turkey *Kalkun*
Onion *Løg*	Rice *Ris*	Vanilla *Vanille*
Orange *Appelsin*	Ring *Kranse*	Vegetable *Grønstag*
Oven *Stegeovn*	Roast *Steg, Riste*	Venison *Dyrekød*
Oyster *Øster*	Rusks *Skorpor*	Waffle *Vaffel*
Pan *Pande*	Rye *Rug*	Walnut *Valnød*
Pancakes *Pandekager*	Salad *salat*	Warm *Varm*
Parsley *Persil*	Salad oil *Madolie*	Water *Vand*
Partridge *Agerhøne*	Salmon *Laks*	Wheat *Hvede*
Pastry *Bagværk*	Salt *Salt*	Whipped Cream *Flødeskum*
Pâté *Postej*	Saltshaker *Saltkar*	Wine *Vin*
Pea *Aerte*	Sardine *Sardin*	Yolk *Æggeblomme*
Peach *Fersken*	Sauce *Sovs*	

Index

Also by Arthur L. Meyer

Corsican Cuisine: Flavors from the Perfumed Isle

"Art Meyer's *Corsican Cuisine* does a superb job of opening the door to this hearty, undiscovered cuisine by providing simple, rustic recipes that capture the essence of Mediterranean peasant cooking at its best."

—Bruce Aidells, Co-author, *The Complete Meat Cookbook*

Savor the unique tastes of Corsica, where basic cooking techniques pair with fresh ingredients to create complex flavors in simple and satisfying fare. Try your hand at traditional staples like Garlic Soup, Ragout of Game Hen with Myrtle, and Wild Boar Meatballs with Roasted Red Peppers. Or satisfy your sweet tooth with Chestnut Beignets and Sweet Cheese-Filled Turnovers. Meyer provides an invaluable resource for the foods of the perfumed isle, including 100 authentic and easy-to-follow Corsican recipes, a 16-page color photo insert, and a glossary of Corsican foods and culinary terms.

121 pages • ISBN 978-0-7818-1248-1 • $35.00hc

More Danish Interest Titles from Hippocrene Books

Beginner's Danish with 2 Audio CDs
Nete Schmidt

This beginner's guide to the Danish language presents basic grammar, vocabulary, and common phrases in 13 clear, concise lessons. It includes topics such as greetings, family, athletics, dining, illness, and holidays. Vocabulary lists, explanations of grammar, and exercises follow each dialogue section, and the audio CDs provide oral and listening comprehension practice. Also included are Danish-English and English-Danish glossaries, as well as an introduction to Danish history and culture.

ISBN 978-0-7818-1199-6 • $29.95pb

Danish-English/English-Danish Dictionary & Phrasebook
5,000 entries • ISBN 0-7818-0917-7 • $13.95pb

Danish-English/English-Danish Practical Dictionary
32,000 entries • ISBN 0-87052-823-8 • $16.95pb

Other Scandinavian Interest Titles

Beginner's Finnish with 2 Audio CDs
ISBN 0-7818-1228-3 • $29.95pb

Finnish-English/English-Finnish Concise Dictionary
12,000 entries • ISBN 0-87052-813-0 • $14.95pb

Finnish-English/English-Finnish Dictionary & Phrasebook
5,000 entries • ISBN 0-7818-0956-8 • $13.95pb

The Best of Finnish Cooking *—Taimi Previdi*
ISBN 0-7818-0493-0 • $12.95pb

Beginner's Icelandic with 2 Audio CDs
ISBN 978-0-7818-1191-0 • $29.95pb

Icelandic-English/English-Icelandic Concise Dictionary
10,000 entries • ISBN 0-87052-801-7 • $12.95pb

Beginner's Norwegian with 2 Audio CDs
ISBN 0-7818-1043-4 • $26.95pb

Hippocrene Children's Illustrated Norwegian Dictionary
500 entries • ISBN 978-0-7818-0887-3 • $14.95pb

Norwegian-English/English-Norwegian Dictionary & Phrasebook
3,500 entries • ISBN 0-7818-0955-X • $13.95pb

Norwegian-English/English-Norwegian Practical Dictionary
50,000 entries • ISBN 978-0-7818-1106-4 • $24.95pb

Beginner's Swedish with 2 Audio CDs
ISBN 0-7818-1157-0 • $29.95pb

Hippocrene Children's Illustrated Swedish Dictionary
500 entries • ISBN 978-0-7818-0850-7 • $14.95pb

Swedish-English/English-Swedish Dictionary & Phrasebook
3,000 entries • ISBN 0-7818-0903-7 • $11.95pb

Swedish-English/English-Swedish Practical Dictionary
28,000 entries • ISBN 978-0-7818-1246-7 • $29.95pb

Sweden: An Illustrated History *—Martina Sprague*
234 pages • ISBN 0-7818-1114-7 • $14.95pb

Norse Warfare: Unconventional Battle Strategies of the Ancient Vikings *—Martina Sprague*
350 pages • ISBN 0-7818-1176-7 • $29.95hc

Prices subject to change without prior notice. **To purchase Hippocrene Books** contact your local bookstore, visit www.hippocrenebooks.com, call (212) 685-4373, or write to: HIPPOCRENE BOOKS, 171 Madison Avenue, New York, NY 10016.